RELIGION AND THE ROMANS

Roman worshipper burning incense: is this the Genius depicted as the paterfamilias?

Classical World series

RELIGION AND THE ROMANS

Ken Dowden

Bristol Classical Press

General Editor: John H. Betts

This impression 2007
First published in 1992 by
Bristol Classical Press
an imprint of
Gerald Duckworth & Co. Ltd.
90-93 Cowcross Street, London EC1M 6BF
Tel: 020 7490 7300
Fax: 020 7490 0080
inquiries@duckworth-publishers.co.uk
www.ducknet.co.uk

Reprinted 1995, 1997, 1998, 2000, 2001

© 1992 by Ken Dowden

A catalogue record for this book is available
from the British Library

ISBN 978 1 85399 180 6

Contents

List of Illustrations   vi

Preface   vii

1. Religion, Ancient   1

2. Old Rome   12

3. The Controlled Republic   31

4. Empire and Provinces   45

5. New Wave   65

6. Christian Toleration   80

Suggestions for Further Study   91

Suggestions for Further Reading   93

Ancient Sources and Inscriptions Quoted   97

Index of Key Terms   102

List of Illustrations

I am profoundly grateful to the institutions credited below for their unhesitating permission to reproduce these photographs in this book.

Frontispiece Roman worshipper burning incense (Genius?)
Bronze figurine, 16.7 cm. Musée de la Civilisation Gallo-Romaine, Lyon (inv. bronzes 73)

p. 20 A *Lupercus*
Photo, copyright: Monumenti Musei e Gallerie Pontificie, Vatican City (Galleria Lapidaria inv. 9312; neg. xxxii. 38.31)

p. 29 Cult of the Lares Augusti, depicted on an altar set up by a *vicomagister.* Palazzo dei Conservatori, Rome.
Photo, copyright: Deutsches archaeologisches Institut, Rome (neg. 60 1472)

p. 38 Sarcophagus with characteristic Dionysiac scene. National Archaeological Museum, Naples.
Photo, copyright: Soprintendenza alle antichità delle province di Napoli e Caserta, Naples (inv. 6726; neg. 704)

p. 51 The Mercury of Lezoux (near Clermont-Ferrand). Musée des Antiquités nationales, St Germain-en-Laye (near Paris).
Photo, copyright: Réunion des Musées Nationaux, Paris (inv. MAN 46276; neg. 88EN7032)

p. 70 Isis as one of her worshippers. National Archaeological Museum, Naples.
Photo, copyright: Soprintendenza alle antichità delle province di Napoli e Caserta, Naples (inv. 6372; neg. 2939)

p. 77 The Mithraic Lion grade. Palazzo Colonna, Rome.
Photo, copyright: Deutsches archaeologisches Institut, Rome (neg. 33 1718)

Preface

Roman religion is a huge subject and this book is short. I have included much of what I think matters, though there are some subjects I regret leaving out: philosophical thought about god and man, and sub-religious practices – particularly astrology and magic. All chapters are to an extent skeletal – they are samplers of this period or that aspect, and some more than others, as the reader will find when he or she comes to Roman Britain or Christianity. But I think that tastes will be whetted.

In ancient religion we can take very different views of what is important. The knowledgeable reader may be surprised not to find these topics:

Functions of the various gods:
I have seen no point in writing pretty paragraphs about e.g. Neptune being god of the sea. This doesn't do much more than describe Greek mythology in Roman dress and is not the business of this book. Anyone who wants this information should look in the *Oxford Classical Dictionary.*

The Roman calendar:
I do not have room to plod month by month through the Roman calendar and have some doubts about the usefulness of doing so. It is done well in any case by H.H. Scullard, *Festivals and Ceremonies of the Roman Republic.* For the severe limits on our knowledge of the significance of the Roman festival system, see chap. 2, p. 24.

Numen:
Some writers have argued (and more have unthinkingly repeated) that the Romans perceived a mysterious power immanent in things, like the Polynesian *mana* (which is also a misrepresentation of Polynesian thought!) and suppose that the Romans called this power *numen*. It is then supposed that the Romans themselves had evolved from a primitive religion only aware of vague powers to a more advanced

conception of gods like men ('anthropomorphism'), as though the Romans had passed in a few hundred years through the entire religious evolution of man. In fact, the Romans were nowhere near the beginnings of religion and had anthropomorphic religion from their Indo-European roots. The interpretation of *numen* in this way is wholly mistaken.

Ken Dowden
The University of Birmingham
1991

Chapter 1
Religion, Ancient

At 9am on a Saturday morning in September 1984 a peaceful London suburb witnessed an alarming scene:

> Residents said that several men pulled a live sheep from a house in the gardens and were followed by an Iranian priest. The animal's throat was cut and the blood was allowed to run into a drain. The dead sheep was taken back to the house.
>
> *Sunday Telegraph*, 23 September 1984

As a neighbour reported: 'Two men held the struggling animal with its head over the drain. A man then appeared with a watering can and water was sprinkled over the sheep's head. Another man, wearing what seemed like a butcher's coat, cut its neck with a long knife.' And Mr David Mellor, MP for Putney (who later went on to become a minister for culture), denounced 'an outrageous and barbaric incident', whilst further residents complained that the killing could have been seen by children and that 'It's not the sort of thing that happens in Roehampton – or anywhere else, for that matter – on a Saturday morning.'

A Roman would have been astonished. Blood sacrifice was at the heart of Roman religion and of almost every religion of the ancient world. Without butchery there could be no piety. Indeed, if he found any fault with this scene, other than the strange lack of provision for butchery in the garden, it would be that the blood was wasted: why was it not collected as it spurted out of the dying animal and poured over the god's altar? That is what Lucretius describes – though he is condemning what everyone else does:

> 1.1 Nor is it any piety frequently to be seen, head covered, turning to a (sacred) stone and advancing towards every altar; or to fall face to the ground and stretch out one's hands before the gods' shrines; or to shower the altars with the copious blood of oxen; or to heap vow upon vow.
>
> LUCRETIUS, *Nature of the Universe* 5.1197-1201

1

Blood sacrifice (the sacrifice of animals) was practised by the vast majority of mankind in the ancient world. Only a few outlandish categories rejected it:

* Epicureans like Lucretius, because it was pointless; also some Stoics.
* Pythagorean philosophers who believed in reincarnation and worried that the animal they killed and ate might be a dead relative in his or her next existence.
* The naked philosophers, the 'Gymnosophists' of India, a class of Brahmans at the fringes of the known world (the predecessors of Buddhist and other ascetic holy men who still draw our attention today).
* The Christians, not for any love of animals or queasiness at slaughter, but because (oddly) they could not be defiled by the meat slaughtered to other gods.

Even for Christianity, sacrifice and tasting the victim is central – but its meaning has changed and further blood sacrifice has become obsolete:

> 1.2 ...we are sanctified through the offering of the body of Jesus Christ once and for all. And whilst every priest stands daily performing ritual, time and again offering the same sacrifices, which can never take away sins, he himself [Jesus], after offering one sacrifice for sins for ever, took his seat at God's right hand.
>
> PAUL, *Hebrews* 10.10-12

So when (chap. 6, p. 86) the Emperor Decius issued an edict requiring everyone in the Empire to sacrifice to the gods, it became a test above all for Christians, isolating them in their impious refusal to shed animal blood to the gods, something no respectable and god-fearing person would hesitate to do. What after all would be the result of deliberately refusing to honour the gods? Ordinary people felt that this peculiar impiety of the Christians had resulted in the bitter tragedies of earthquakes and famines. That was the punishment inflicted by angry gods – and it was one reason, maybe the most important, for the persecution of the Christians.

Giving keeps the 'peace'

Gifts are never routine. Their power was felt especially strongly in ancient, traditional societies. The purpose of a gift to the gods, as of gifts to anyone, is to please the person who receives it, so maintaining or strengthening your relationship with them and (if occasion arises) making them feel they owe you a favour – as these slightly tongue-in-cheek lines show:

> 1.3 Gifts, believe me, win over both men and gods:
> Giving gifts keeps Jupiter himself content.
>
> OVID, *Art of Love* 3.653-4

This attitude is sometimes described as *do ut des* ('I give so that you may give'), but that focuses too much on the hope of a future gift and too little on the relationship and bond which my gift establishes here and now.

Most prayers envisage no specific gift:

> 1.4 ...for this purpose, in sacrificing this pig as a *piaculum*, I pray proper prayers to you, that you may be willing and favourable to me, my house, my household [*familia*] and my children.
>
> CATO, *On Agriculture* 139

A *piaculum* is an offering, typically of a pig, to restore good relations with a god: English authors use words like 'expiation' and 'atonement' to catch its flavour. But Romans are all too ready to believe that relations need to be restored: their religion can be cautious, to say the least. Consider too what the alternative is to a 'willing and favourable' god – that is why the Romans set so much store by the *pax deorum* ('peace with the gods'), a sort of treaty which the gods had to be encouraged to sign.

> 1.5 Both that year and the following year – the consulship of Gaius Sulpicius Peticus and Gaius Licinius Stolo [364 BC] – there was a plague. Nothing worth recording was done during the year, except for the performance of a *lectisternium* [chap. 3, pp. 32-3] for the third time in Rome's history in order to beg for the *pax deorum*.
>
> LIVY 7.2.2

Gifts to the gods take many forms.

* Articles of particular value or significance: paintings,

weapons, clothing – perhaps in some way appropriate to the circumstances which bring about your gift to the god. Such things are usually kept in the god's temple, for instance hung on its walls.

* The very temple of the god must once have been built as a gift, an expensive one such as states, emperors or millionaires make. And the land on which it is built was once itself given over (made *sacrum* – below, pp. 5-6) to the god.

* Statues are a lasting and costly present, as pleasing to gods as they are to civic worthies. But they also present a way of visualising the god and enhance contact and communication between god and man.

* Particularly frequent are food and drink offerings. Domestic gifts above all might be simple: fruit, cheese, grain – 'salted meal' (*mola salsa*) was a special recipe, prepared by Vestal Virgins amongst others – honey and milk, or wine, might often be poured. Varro fondly imagined, following philosophical speculation, that in earliest times all offerings had been of this sort.

* Blood sacrifice: the standard offering and a particularly powerful gift, offering a life (or many) to the gods, the warm blood to their altars. Afterwards there is food for men to eat in the company of gods who savour the aroma. This more than anything else got through to the gods.

Give gladly

The attitude of the giver matters. Frequently on *inscriptions* (see below, p. 10) it is stressed that the gift is given *lubens*, 'of one's own free will', and the adverb *merito*, 'deservedly', marks one's full appreciation of the god:

> 1.6 Publius Pomponius son of Numerius gave this gift freely [*lubens*] to Angitia [a Marsian goddess, good against poisonous snakes – Vergil, *Aeneid* 7.759] and deservedly [*merito*].
> INSCRIPTION (early, Italian), *CIL* I² 1763

The word 'freely' contrasts with the trouble and expense of the gift – the gift must be in our sense too a 'sacrifice'. If you pay for it out of your pocket, you mention that to stress your devotion. The following is clearly expensive – it is written in verse:

1.7 Marcus and Publius Vertuleius, sons of Gaius.
Whereas their father, being worried and upset at the grim
state of his finances, made a vow here, his children after the
fulfilment of the vow, giving a sacred meal with 10 per cent
of the proceeds, gladly give a gift to Hercules, most certainly deservedly. At the same time they beg you [Hercules]
to condemn them often to such a vow.

INSCRIPTION, *CIL* X 5708

This comes from a shrine of Hercules at Sora, in the mountains 90 km
SE of Rome, and dates back to the second century BC. It shows the
practical application of religion in cases of personal difficulty. The
Vertulei are obviously prominent members of their community.

You can also get some feel for Roman religion from abbreviations found useful in inscriptions:

SOME ABBREVIATIONS IN RELIGIOUS INSCRIPTIONS

	Stands for	*Means*
DD	DONUM/DONO DEDIT	Gave (this) gift/as a gift
D	DEDICAVIT	Dedicated, gave this gift
F	FECIT	Built/made
FC	FIERI CURAVIT	Caused to be built/made
LDDD	LOCUS DATUS DECRETO	Land provided by
	DECURIONUM	the city council
L	LIBENS or LUBENS	Of (the giver's) free will
M	MERITO	Deservedly (of the god)
LL	LAETUS LIBENS	Happily and freely
PPP	PRO PIETATE POSUIT	Deposited (the gift) out of piety
or	PECUNIA PROPRIA POSUIT	Deposited (the gift) at his own expense
DS	DE SUO	At (the giver's) own expense
SP	SUA PECUNIA	Out of (the giver's) own money
VS	VOTO SOLUTO	In payment of (the giver's) vow
or	VOTUM SOLVIT	Paid one's vow
IOM	IOVI OPTIMO MAXIMO	To Jupiter Best and Greatest
DM	DIS MANIBUS	To the departed spirits of (so-and-so)
S(AC)	SACER/SACRUM	Sacred (property)

Sacer, which gives us our word 'sacred', marks something as divine property: something given to Jupiter is IOVI SACRUM. In the fullest sense, the ancient lawyers are right that 'a thing can only be considered *sacrum* if it has been consecrated with the authority of the Roman People, e.g. when a law on it has been passed or a decree of the Senate made' (GAIUS, *Institutes* 2.5). Other things were merely *religiosum* – imbued with *religio*, not 'religion', but the need to watch your religious step. *Religio* is careful observance with some prohibition lurking in the background. But the lawyers were being pedantic: graves (which you should respect and leave alone), technically only *religiosum*, are still marked 'DMS':

1.8   DMS

Lucius Valerius Fyrmus son of Lucius

Priest of Isis of Ostia

And of the Mother of the Gods on the Left Bank (Transtiberina)

Made this for himself.

INSCRIPTION, *CIL* XIV 429

If you give grain or sacrifice you make (*fac-*) it *sacer* – this action of giving is therefore what is meant by *sacrificium*. But if a person is made '*sacer*', this is not to make them holy, it is to deliver them and their property to the gods – in effect to 'sacrifice' them. An ancient law stated, 'If a patron defrauds his client, let him be *sacer*' (*Law of the Twelve Tables*, Table viii, fr. 21). And when Cicero returned from exile in 57 BC not only had his house been burnt down by his political enemies, it had also been confiscated – i.e. consecrated, made *sacrum*. Fortunately, however, he 'discovered' that the ritual of consecration had been incorrectly carried out and so, after legal argument before the *pontifices* (chap. 2, p. 18), could repossess the land.

Sacrifice now!

There are three occasions for sacrifice and gifts:

1. To ask for help
2. To thank the god for help received
3. To celebrate a regular occasion, simply to honour the god

1. Asking for help, or praying, is not by itself enough to ensure the help of a god. Ancient gods have no interest in whether you will mend your ways and lead a better life: they need a more substantial offering. Only a gift, typically a sacrifice, will make the gods listen to your prayer

(though whether they do anything about it is up to them). Prayer without payment is invalid, though payment by credit card (or Cash On Delivery) is allowed in extreme circumstances: you may vow, for instance, that if you reach dry land without drowning you will sacrifice this or give that. The gift to Hercules of the brothers Vertulei was of this type.

2. Thanking the god for help is usually related to an earlier request. A record of payment of a vow is today called an *ex voto* – like the plaques in Catholic churches saying MERCI or GRAZIE. Ancient inscriptions were fuller:

> 1.9 to...and to Isis health-giver, for the health of Quintus Vergilius Modestus his mother Cassia made this dedication in payment of her vow.
>
> INSCRIPTION, *CIL* VI 436

3. Asking and thanking are always exceptional. Normally individuals, households, communities, cities and states are engaged in a continuous recognition of the importance of gods. No meal time will pass without an offering to the household gods, the *Penates*. On the birthday of the head of the household there will be offerings to his *Genius*. And in both countryside and city there will be frequent festivals. At state temples the god will expect an annual gift of festival with sacrifice: the state calendars scrupulously marked the 'birthdays' of temples, i.e. the dates on which they were dedicated, for just that purpose.

Sacrifice was the focus of festivals, and games and entertainments were an inseparable part of the celebration. Late emperors, intent on abolishing paganism and banning its sacrifices, had to make a new distinction between sacred and secular in order to preserve the entertainments and the great public temple-buildings around which they took place. Festivals in turn determined the rhythm of the year. Our year is given a shape by weeks and by public holidays whose origin in 'holy days' is often visible (even if the 'secularisation' of Christmas is frequently lamented). The Romans might have understood these holidays, but until the third or fourth century AD, the week and the idea of named days of the week were unknown to them. The week is dependent on the Christian and Jewish custom of regularly observing the seventh day (the sabbath) as a holy day. The only comparable rhythm in the Roman calendar was the market day (*nundinae*), held every eighth day – and that would not apply in say Greece, Egypt or Gaul.

The faith of the Romans?

One of the hardest features of ancient religion for the modern student is the sheer unimportance of belief. We live in a world of creeds and -isms and when we first meet a new religion, we naturally ask 'what do they believe?' We even refer to modern religions as 'living faiths'. The ancient religions, however, are not dead faiths: they are obsolete practices. Most Romans (and inhabitants of the provinces too) were engaged, in their varying local ways, in maintaining the *pax deorum*, by correct observance of rituals at important points in the year and in their lives, and strove to give the gods the honour due to them. They were unworried by souls and afterlives (except that the dead needed placation), reckoned their moral behaviour was up to them and what others thought of them, and had no notion that they needed to be 'saved' from anything – other than bad harvests, disease and childlessness.

With belief goes choice: few radical religious choices were made in antiquity. Roman religion was not a personally chosen, truer, more correct religion: it was simply the religious tradition which Romans practised, whilst respecting the rights of other nations to follow their own traditions (chap. 4, p. 44). This helps to explain why Romans tolerated Judaism (these were the practices of the Jewish nation, scattered though it was), but abhorred Christians (who had deliberately rejected national traditions in favour of impiety).

As there was no set of required beliefs, it is not really surprising that there were no scriptures or sacred texts (other than some copies of hymns and rituals). What perhaps is odd is that in the strict sense there is not even any Roman mythology. The mythology used by the Roman poets and passed down to the modern day is in fact Greek, with Greek names for gods changed to Latin (so Diana instead of Artemis, Venus instead of Aphrodite, Jupiter instead of Zeus). In the distant past the Romans had once had a mythology, but by the time of our sources it has been converted into the 'history' of early Rome and can only be converted back into mythology by complex and disputable methods.

Belief only became important for small, untypical sectors of the population, though they were energetic and visible enough. We may think of the tiny minority who personally chose to become devotees of exotic religions, such as Isis and Mithras. Or perhaps we think of philosophers, a vocal and visible minority in Greek cities, but of course unknown in the countryside or in the non-urban provinces (making a British philosopher a contradiction in terms). That did not stop philosophers from being divided into several different 'schools' (i.e. sects) – Platonists ('Academics'), Peripatetics, Stoics, Epicureans, Sceptics.

A final, grossly untypical, minority was the Roman aristocracy – an elite in an economically inefficient, pre-industrial world, living off the meagre surplus production of the rest of the population. They lived comfortably in Rome (and their villas in the countryside) and had the leisure to write literature. For them the simple practice of religion was not enough: they needed ideas too and drew them from Greek philosophers, whose lectures they could attend in Athens after finishing their basic education in Italy. They would find it important to make choices: to choose a philosophy was to select your image of yourself. Cato the Younger was an unbending Stoic, a role he played with genius and consistency up to and including his suicide at Utica in 46 BC. Caesar was a no-nonsense Epicurean. Cicero was, in his own eyes, a liberal and fair-minded 'eclectic' (which means he selected what he thought best from different schools, mainly Stoic and Platonist). It was philosophers who speculated about the nature of the soul and of the gods and of the good life. Cicero's *On the Nature of the Gods* tells us practically nothing about Roman religion, but plenty about Greek philosophy.

The vast majority of the population was content if the gods received their traditional worship and if the rhythm of the year continued to be underlined by festivals, performed well and enjoyably. Somewhere beyond these classes, usually in cities, lay the floating voters of ancient religion, those whose susceptible natures were attracted by the promise of something new or something powerful: to them you could sell an interpretation of their last dream, or a spell for wreaking awful vengeance on *every* part of their enemy's body. They might be impressed by swirling dancing, flagellation, secret rites performed in murky but cosmic cellars, by fancy dress, by foreign languages and by miracles.

What we know and how we know it

It would be easy (and dull) if Roman religion – or any other part of the history of mankind – was just a database which you printed out in books like this. Obviously there are many questions about the Romans that we cannot answer because there are gaps in the data. But there is a more important problem: what do we actually want to know about

Roman religion? Every book has its own view about which questions to ask. I have concentrated on areas where we can get some 'feel' for religion and society, rather than on amassing points of knowledge that will make the reader a quiz champion ('At what Roman festival were pregnant sows sacrificed?'). But even here there is no fixed list of which topics matter.

There is, however, a more or less fixed list of areas from which we can derive information about Roman religion:

1. *Archaeology*

* Silent remains: temples (maybe only their foundations), shrines, precincts. Not, of course, sacred trees (bio-degradable). Pools with skulls in them. Cult implements, gifts.
* Things which depict: statues, statuettes, frescoes, sculptures on columns or on altars, coins.
* Written remains: papyrus (ancient paper) is perishable and only survives in quantity in Egypt – written in Greek. For the Latin West, inscriptions are the only extensive source. An *inscription* is simply writing carved onto stone, designed to accompany a dedication, to proclaim, or to record.

2. *Literature*

Amazingly, many of the writings of Greeks and Romans have been read and copied continuously over a period of 2000 years and never wholly lost. Yet little of what survives is about Roman religion. Our surviving sources are:

* Romans (and Greeks) writing about religion. Few did, and few of their works actually survive: Ovid's *Fasti* or Plutarch's (Greek) work *On Isis and Osiris* are important sources – though the latter is more on ideas than cult practices. Writers that survive sometimes quote writings that are lost: most important is Varro's *Human and Divine Antiquities* (chap. 2, pp. 14-15).
* Writers who at some point happen to talk about, deal with, or reveal details of religion, e.g. the historian Livy, or Vergil in his epic the *Aeneid*, or the gorgeous description of a festival of Isis in the last book of Apuleius' novel, *The Golden Ass*.

* Philosophers expounding their preferred system of philosophy, for instance Seneca in his *Moral Letters*, or the Emperor Marcus Aurelius' *Meditations*. But is philosophy religion?

We construct our picture out of a large number of tiny pieces of information – a picture of religions and religious attitudes which differ markedly from each other and to which we will have varying reactions: the quaint, the folksy, the earthy, the solemn, the ceremonious, the hypocritical, the exotic, the trivial, the superficial, the deep, the mystical, the solitary, the companionable, the military, the maternal, the philosophical and the fraudulent. Every type of life in a thousand years of Rome was reflected in religion. Atheism alone gets no look-in.

Chapter 2
Old Rome

Rome was the first point from the sea at which the River Tiber could be crossed and was bound to attract a variety of peoples. The Latins (whose language Rome spoke) are just one tribe that settled there. Traditionally there were Sabines too, a related tribe, but with some variations in language and culture. And Rome also attracted the Etruscans, a mysterious people: we have too little Etruscan writing left to understand their language or origins. But their culture developed earlier than that of the Latins and it was the Etruscans who first brought Greek culture (including the alphabet) to Rome. Indeed the name of the last king of Rome, Tarquin the Proud (Tarquinius Superbus), is Etruscan.

It is one of the most remarkable facts in history that this well-sited trading centre became the leader of an empire which, at its greatest extent, stretched from modern Portugal in the West to Turkey and Armenia in the East, from Britain in the North West to Egypt in the South East. Yet the Romans were not a *nation*, like the Sumerians, Assyrians, Persians, Egyptians or Chinese, but a mere city. So whose religion is 'Roman religion'? I have made a choice: during the Republic, we will look mainly at the city of Rome; during the Empire, however, 'Roman religion' will mean the religion of the provinces also. Other choices could have been made: it would be interesting to learn about the religion of Italy during the Republic – though evidence is thin; or we could have told a more continuous story by only considering the governing class at Rome – though this would be unfair to the other 99.9 per cent!

Prehistory: Indo-European, Italic, Etruscan

Latin, the language of Rome and the Latins, which survives today as French, Spanish, Italian, etc., was a sister language to most of the languages of Europe, e.g. Greek, the Celtic languages (e.g. Welsh), the Slavonic languages (e.g. Russian) and the Germanic languages (e.g. English). The similarity of 'father' to *pater*, 'three' to *tres*, 'me' to *me* is no coincidence. Latin descends from the same original language as English, the *Indo-European* language spoken before 3000 BC by our common ancestors when they perhaps lived north of the Black Sea. The Indo-European peoples migrated, and their language and customs gradually changed as time passed and as they lived amongst peoples of other cultures. The Romans were closer than us to their Indo-European origins and maintained some aspects of Indo-European society and religion. Notably, the father of the family – the *paterfamilias* whose *genius* the Roman household worshipped – had great authority (it was very much a *patriarchal* society). And the chief god was a corresponding 'father of gods and of men', whose name survives in various Indo-European languages:

Latin	Greek	Sanskrit	English
Juppiter	*Zeus pater*	*Dyāuḥ pitaḥ*	*Tues*(day)

His name is connected with the daytime sky: he is a 'sky father'. On earth, a corresponding religious authority perhaps belonged to the Roman king (chap. 4, p. 57), as it had to his Indo-European forebears. But there is little which can easily be traced to the Indo-European heritage: the importance of the hearth (and of fire in general, tended by (Vestal) virgins), horse-sacrifice, and the strange (not quite neuter) word for priest, *flamen*, apparently the same word as the Sanskrit *brahman*.

The Indo-European tribes that came to Italy are called the 'Italic' tribes, and probably shared their own version of Indo-European culture, maybe around 2000/1500 BC: Mars, the warrior god, must have emerged at this time, and Diana – a female of Indo-European *Dyēus like the Greek Dione – may now have acquired her prominence. Our knowledge of this period is slight.

Once Rome was founded (and maybe before) the Latin subdivision of the Italic tribes interacted with the (non-Indo-European) Etruscans, who had a formative influence on Roman religion and national identity. The first great, Greek-style temple in Rome (maybe the first temple at all) was being built by King Tarquin on the Capitol Hill as he was expelled (traditional date: 509 BC). And the (religious) calendar appears to owe at least two months to the Etruscans: 'April' is named after an Etruscanised version of the Greek goddess Aphrodite; and 'June' (*Junius*) should have been 'Junone' if it had come from the Latin goddess Juno.

Getting at the past: Varro to the rescue

Old Rome is almost beyond the reach of history. The Kingdom (traditionally, 753-509 BC) existed long before any Latin authors or inscriptions and our knowledge of it is a matter of deduction, inference and hearsay. Even our knowledge of the Republic switches in late: what we really know about is Roman high society and politics from the 60s BC onwards. Can we say anything about the earliest Roman religion? At first sight the situation looks bleak:

* Before 90 BC the only authors to survive are the comic play-wrights Plautus and Terence.
* Of the early writers that are lost (apart from a few snippets) none wrote before the 240s BC.
* Record-keeping was primitive by our standards, and memory of past events in family traditions aimed to polish the family image, not to preserve accurate information.
* Only 1.4 per cent of Latin inscriptions date from the Republic. Only a handful date from before 200 BC.
* Archaeology has little to tell us about the religion of the Kingdom or the early Republic. Even Cicero's Rome has largely disappeared thanks to constant redevelopment in antiquity.

However, we are not alone: some Roman writers of the late Republic felt that ancient religious traditions were slipping from their grasp and did something about it – above all, Rome's greatest scholar, M. Terentius Varro, a man 10 years older than Cicero, 16 years older than Caesar, in his hugely influential masterpiece, the *Human and Divine Antiquities*. He completed the work in 47 BC and dedicated it to the Pontifex Maximus – Caesar. Though the loss of this work is one of the major tragedies in the study of Roman religion, we know a great deal about it as later authors quote it in detail. In particular, St Augustine, whilst writing his *City of God* to show Christianity had not been to blame for the sack of Rome in AD 410 and launching a counter-attack on traditional paganism, preserves much of Varro and much about traditional paganism that would otherwise be lost.

Varro wrote 20 books on *Human Antiquities*, before proceeding in the second part to the 16 books of the *Divine Antiquities*, where he dealt with religion in this way:

1		General
2-4	PEOPLE.	Priests: Pontifices, Augurs, Board of 15
5-7	PLACES.	Shrines, temples, religious sites
8-10	TIMES.	Festivals, games, theatrical performances
11-13	THINGS.	Consecrations, and rites private and public
14-16	GODS.	Gods understood by Varro, gods not wholly understood, and the principal, select, gods

'Antiquities'? Parts of the religion that Varro was describing had fallen into decay leaving quaint remnants and relics to amaze Roman aristocrats brought up on Greek philosophy. Varro himself in his introduction wrote as follows:

> 2.1 I fear the gods may perish not by attack from outside, but through the indifference of Roman citizens – a disaster from which I rescue them: by this sort of book they are stored and preserved in the memory of respectable people, an effort more useful than Metellus' rescue of the holies of Vesta from the fire [as Pontifex Maximus in 241 BC – he was blinded in the process] or Aeneas' rescue of the Penates from the destruction of Troy [Vergil, *Aeneid* e.g. 2.717, 3.12].
> VARRO, *Divine Antiquities* 1 fr. 2a (= AUGUSTINE, *City of God*, 6.2)

This was no exaggeration – Varro figures as a character in one of Cicero's dialogues and gets this support:

> 2.2 'What you say, Varro, is true,' I replied. 'We were wandering and straying about like strangers in our own city, and your books led us, so to speak, right home: at last we could realise who and where we were. You have revealed the age of our native city, the chronology of its history, the laws of its religion and its priesthood, its civil and military institutions, the topography of its districts and its sites, the terminology, classification and moral and rational basis of all our religious and secular institutions...'
> CICERO, *Academica* 1.3 (9)

Varro's work was typical of the times. An attempt to solve current problems by returning to the original good health of Roman traditions, which we later see in full flower in Augustus' policies and writers such as Livy and Vergil, began with the antiquarianism and idealism of the 50s of which Varro was a part. At much the same time,

Nigidius Figulus was writing a long work, in 20 volumes or more, *On the Gods*. And Cicero's own *On the Nature of the Gods*, in a mere 3 volumes (167 Penguin pages) followed around 45 BC. Later, M. Verrius Flaccus wrote a work on the rites found in the Roman calendar, which, like Varro, was of use to Ovid in writing his *Fasti*. This was a poem running through the old-fashioned Roman religious year, though he only got as far as June before he was exiled.

Personnel

The ancient priesthoods
The Emperor Augustus, in AD 13, the year before he died, was proud to state in his list of achievements:

> 2.3 I have been Pontifex Maximus, Augur, XVvir for Conducting the Rites, VIIvir Epulo, an Arval Brother, a Sodalis Titius, a Fetialis.
>
> AUGUSTUS, *Res Gestae* 7

The first four in the list were the four colleges of priests in his day.

1. *The VIIviri Epulones*: viri means 'men' and you call a board of 7 men 'the Sevenmen' – VIIviri (*septemviri* in full). A member of the board, like Augustus, is a 'Sevenman'. These 'Sevenmen Banqueters' were introduced fairly late, in 196 BC, to assist the *Pontifices* with arrangements for sacrifices (and therefore feasts) which were becoming ever more numerous, especially with the new rites introduced by the *Xviri Sacris Faciundis* (see below). Numbers: IIIviri 196 BC; VIIviri maybe 81 BC. Caesar temporarily increased the number of this college as of the others in 47/44 BC. They ranked fourth in the hierarchy of colleges.

2. The *XVviri Sacris Faciundis* ('Fifteenmen for Conducting the Rites') were originally maybe only administrative assistants, but in historical times managed the introduction of Greek-style rites on the basis of the Sibylline Books (chap. 3, p. 32). Numbers: IIviri in '509' BC; Xviri, 367 BC; XVviri, 81 BC. They ranked third, and unlike other major religious institutions were *not* supposed to have been created by King Numa, the (mythical) second King of Rome, but by the Tarquins.

3. The *Augurs* were indeed invented by 'King Numa' – making them an ancient part of Roman religion, as is confirmed by the presence of *augures* in other Italian cities too. Numbers: 3 in '509' BC (i.e. one per tribe); 9 in 300 BC; 15 in 81 BC. They ranked second of the colleges.

The augurs are not strictly priests. They are, rather, official experts on *auguria* ('auguries' in English) – signs encouraging or discouraging a proposed course of action. An approved action is *fas*, religiously permitted. The opposite is *nefas*, an offence against religion. *Auspicia* ('auspices' in English) are the usual form of augury and occur when you observe birds and see signs in how they behave. Every magistrate (e.g. the consul Bibulus, chap. 3, pp. 42-3) has the right to observe auguries (*ius augurale*), in particular, the right to take auspices (*ius auspicii*). The augur, however, is only called in as a consultant, whether to perform himself or just to assist and advise. His special emblem is his *lituus* – a staff with its top shaped like our modern question-marks – and he uses it to mark out a *templum* (an area of sky or land). This is the picture presented by Livy when he imagines (in his study in the early 20s BC) the confirmation of Numa as king:

> 2.4 The augur veiled his head and sat on Numa's left, holding in his right hand a bent staff with no knots in it, which they called a *lituus*. Then, looking towards the City and its land, he prayed to the gods and defined the regions from east to west: he stated that the right-hand area was to the south and the left to the north. Opposite, he mentally defined a feature at the furthest point his eyes could reach. Then, transferring the *lituus* to his left hand and placing his right hand on Numa's head, he prayed thus: 'Father Jupiter, if it is *fas* for this Numa Pompilius whose head I hold to be King at Rome, then may you manifest sure signs unto us within those limits which I have made.' Then he specifically stated the auspices which he wished to be sent and when they were sent Numa was declared king and came down from the *templum*.
>
> LIVY 1.18.7-10

4. In contrast to the few specialists, three augurs and *IIviri Sacris Faciundis* who go back to the times of the kings, the *Collegium Pontificum* ('College of Pontiffs') is more numerous and more significant, coming first in priority. It consisted of the following priests, in order of priority:

1. *Rex Sacrorum* ('King of Rites')
2. the *flamines maiores* ('major flamines'):
   - (a) Flamen Dialis (priest of Jupiter)
   - (b) Flamen Martialis (priest of Mars)
   - (c) Flamen Quirinalis (priest of Quirinus)

3. *Pontifex Maximus* ('principal pontiff')
4. other *Pontifices* (4? in '509' BC; 9 in 300 BC; 14 in 81 BC)
5. the twelve *flamines minores* ('minor flamines'), not ranked individually: priests of Carmenta, Ceres, Falacer, Flora, Furrina, Palatua, Pomona, Portunus, Volcanus, Volturnus – and two others whose names have been forgotten!

The *Rex Sacrorum* was created after the abolition of the monarchy to carry out some sacred duties formerly performed by the king. A *flamen* is a priest special to a particular god, as we meet for instance in Greece. But surprisingly no new *flamines* were created during the Republic (until finally Mark Antony became the *flamen* of the deified Julius Caesar). The list of native gods was in that sense closed by the end of the Kingdom. New gods introduced during the Republic were managed by a growing committee of pontiffs, on the basis of Greek rituals recommended by the Xviri to the Senate. The Senate can thus be viewed as the ultimate religious authority and the priests as sacred magistrates.

The name *pontifices* means 'bridge-makers' in Latin, though the Sanskrit equivalent suggests it may originally have meant 'path-makers', and honestly is a puzzle. It looks as though it goes back before the foundation of Rome. They apparently are an advisory committee to the king, a sort of religious Cabinet with the Pontifex Maximus as their Prime Minister. Their growth in importance continued in the Republic, when the Pontifex Maximus, though nominally fourth in the hierarchy, was the chief magistrate, so to speak, of Roman religion (his title was ultimately taken over by the Pope at the end of the fourth century AD). The pontiffs knew religious tradition and were regularly consulted, rather as one might seek a ruling on a point of law from a praetor. They preserved tradition in the *libri pontificales* ('books of the pontiffs'), for instance by recording all the omens and prodigies of each year (statues sweating blood, two-headed calves, raining stones, lightning striking...), and in other respects too maintained a system of sacred law not released to the general public. Their rulings were sought not on *ius* (secular 'law'), but on *fas* (above, p. 17):

> 2.5 I've often heard from my father that no pontifex worth his salt was ignorant of civil *ius*.
> ...what has a pontiff to do with questions of wall-rights or water-rights or with anything at all except matters tied up with religious observance [*religio*]? And how little that is!

It is a question of rituals, I suppose, of vows, of festivals and
of graves and that sort of thing.

CICERO, *Laws* 2.47

One pontiff was enough for an ordinary matter. But wider public
interest might deserve a panel of three. One hears too of rituals being
carried out 'in accordance with the decree of the pontiffs'. It was,
indeed, before these religious judges that Cicero had to plead his case
for the return of his house (chap. 1, p. 6).

Early Rome was male-dominated: only men are members of the
College – there are no priestesses. The six Vestal Virgins (the only
females in the religious system) are represented in the College by the
Pontifex Maximus: he is their father in religion – a reflection maybe
of the king and his daughters. Both officially reside in the *Regia*, the
Royal Palace.

The gods served by the *flamines minores* have faded beyond
recognition: the names of two are wholly lost, and who they all were
is not only unknown to us, but was even unknown to Varro. How can
a religion fail to remember what its gods are gods of? It is no wonder
that Varro saw himself as engaged in rescue archaeology!

Associations

In addition to the colleges of priests acting on behalf of the whole
community, there were also ancient associations (*sodalitates*) devoted
to particular ancestral rites. Such rites, where we know about them
(we know nothing about the *Sodales Titii* to whom Augustus
belonged, see p. 15), were preserved so carefully that they became
fossils. Romans of the early Empire could scarcely understand the
ancient hymns of the *Salii* (the 'Leaping' dancers of Mars and
Quirinus) or the *Fratres Arvales* ('Brethren of the Fields').

We will look at two ceremonies. First, the rite of the *Luperci*
('Wolf'-men), the *Lupercalia*. It is 15 February 44 BC and Mark
Antony, the leader of a newly created *third* team of *Luperci*, the
Luperci Julii, is about to offer Caesar the crown:

> 2.6 It was the festival of the Lupercalia…many of the noble
> youths and magistrates run naked through the city, striking
> bystanders with shaggy thongs in a spirit of amusement and
> hilarity. And many even high-ranking women deliberately
> present their hands for striking just like at school,
> convinced it helps those who are pregnant to have an easy

A *Lupercus*, unclothed, with 'shaggy thong'.

birth and the barren to become pregnant. Caesar was a
spectator at this, sitting on a golden throne at the Rostra,
dressed in triumphal costume. Mark Antony was one of
those running the sacred race – he was consul. So when he
burst into the Forum and the crowd stood apart for him, he
carried a diadem woven with a wreath of laurel and held it
out to Caesar.

PLUTARCH, *Life of Caesar* 61

This is a nice photo-opportunity for Caesar as he is offered the crown:
it has people out, about, and in the right mood. Is it religious? Yes,
because there must have been a sacrifice and the *pax deorum* was
maintained.

We switch now to the grove of the *Dea Dia* out on the Campanian
Road at the fifth milestone from Rome. It is late in May. No one then
or now knows who the Dea Dia was: 'goddess Dia'? 'bright goddess'?
perhaps, they suggested, she was Tellus, 'Earth'. In any case, the Arval
Brethren (*Fratres Arvales*), twelve of the most distinguished men in
Rome, are present in their full regalia – corn-ears and woollen fillets
in their hair – to perform ancient rites, originally designed in less
sophisticated times to ensure the fertility of the fields. A high spot was
the *tripudium*, a dance in triple time performed only by the Salii, the
Arval Brethren and – so it appears – sacred chickens pecking greedily
at corn. This extract is from their careful records for the year AD 218:

2.7 In the grove of the Dea Dia, Alfenius Avitianus, vice-
president, sacrificed 2 piacular pigs at the altar for thinning
the grove and doing the work; there he had the privilege of
sacrificing [i.e. at his own expense] a heifer and thence
returning to the porch sat on the benches...

Then they went into the temple and prayed at the jars and,
opening the doors, threw them down the slope, then sat on
the marble benches and shared bread which was wreathed
in laurel with the assistance of the public attendants. Then
they took the *lumemulia* [pounded thistles, I think]
together with [mashed?] turnips and smeared it over the
[statues of the] goddesses. And the temple was closed and
everyone went out. Then the priests, shut inside, clothes
girt up, taking the books, dividing the song up, did the
tripudium to the following words:
Hey! help us, Lares! Hey! help us, Lares! Hey! help us,
Lares! Nor allow destruction or ruin, Marmar, to reach the
majority. Nor allow destruction or ruin, Marmar, to reach

the majority. Nor allow destruction or ruin, Marmar, to reach the majority.

Be sated, savage Mars, leap the threshold, stand still, ber! ber! Be sated, savage Mars, leap the threshold, stand still, ber! ber! Be sated, savage Mars, leap the threshold, stand still, ber! ber!

Call ye in turn all the Semones [Sowing-spirits]! Call ye in turn all the Semones! Call ye in turn all the Semones!

Hey! help us, Marmor! Hey! help us, Marmor! Hey! help us, Marmor!

Triumpe! [a ritual Hurrah!] Triumpe! Triumpe! Triumpe! Triumpe!

After the tripodation, next the signal was given for the public attendants to enter and take back the books...

INSCRIPTION, *CIL* VI.2104

It perhaps gives the wrong impression of the hymn to translate it: this automatically suggests that it can be understood, something very doubtful when you look at its olde-worlde Latin. Both the hymn and the ceremony indicate the importance for the Roman aristocracy of the punctilious maintenance of religious traditions. It is rather more than the Roman equivalent of Morris-dancing: it too is an element in preserving the fragile *pax deorum*.

Ancient interests

The earliest Roman religion was dominated by men and war, as we can see from the three principal gods – those with *flamines maiores*. Jupiter reflects the all-powerful father of the household, the *pater-familias*. Quirinus (only later identified with Romulus) appears to be the god of adult male citizens (*Quirites*), the warrior community (*Co-vir*); in any case he is a warlike god sharing features with Mars.

Mars, most military of the gods, is most prominent in Rome, as often in Italian cities. But for the Romans he is special: he is their ancestor, the father of Romulus and Remus. The year begins in his month, *Martialis* (March), with ceremonies to dust off weapons, exercise the cavalry on the *Campus Martius* – the Town Moor and ancient training ground of the Romans – wake the god and generally to prepare the army for the campaigning season. The end of the campaigning season is likewise marked by his ceremonies. Even in agriculture prayers are sometimes directed to Mars, not (as is often thought) because he has any direct connection with fertility, but because the power of the army has allowed agriculture to continue uninterrupted. This, according to Georges Dumézil, in his *Archaic Roman Religion*, vol. II, is the significance of the loaves of bread in the sacrifice of the 'October Horse':

> 2.8 *October Horse* is the name given to the horse sacrificed every year to Mars in the month of October on the Campus Martius, the right-hand horse of a victorious chariot team. There used to be no trivial competition between the inhabitants of Subura and the Sacra Via [districts of Rome] for its head, so that the latter might fix it to the wall of the Regia or the former to the Mamilian tower. Its tail is carried to the Regia with such speed that the blood from it drips on the hearth.
>
> FESTUS s.v. *October equus* (178M, 190L)

> 2.9 They used to garland the head of the horse sacrificed on the Ides of October on the Campus Martius with loaves of bread, because this sacrifice was performed on account of the outcome of the crops; and a horse rather than an ox was sacrificed because it is appropriate to war, whereas the ox is appropriate to the production of crops.
>
> PAULUS, *Excerpts from Festus* s.v. *Panibus* (220M, 246L)

This is a state for whom war is a way of life. They even have a special class of priests (needless to say, appointed by 'King Numa'), the 20 *fetiales* whose job it is to declare war on their neighbours (themselves probably with their own *fetiales* in this deadly ritual game of early times). By colourful rites they would ensure they were fighting a *bellum iustum* – a war allowable according to law (*ius*) and therefore liable not only to be won, but to be 'prosperous'. We should think of raids for cattle and women. This goes back to a Rome with no empire, one city amongst others. As empire developed, the Fetial ritual of flinging a spear from your own territory into your neighbour's became progressively more absurd – as Augustus found when he declared war on Cleopatra's Egypt. The *fetiales* are sometimes thought of as diplomats, because they monitor treaties and visit other states to demand 'justice', but it is doubtful whether their role extended beyond ritual legalism. They do not strike one as the pragmatists of yesteryear.

Beyond war, Roman religion had other interests – crops and animals, as we might expect in an agricultural and pastoral society. But perhaps we discover more superstition than expected and a closer concern with the dead. Ovid, a stylish and sophisticated writer, takes particular pleasure in describing an olde-worlde part of the Lemuria festival with its ghosts and mesmeric rites:

> 2.10 It was the month of May – named after our ancestors [maiores!], which even now keeps part of its antique ways: when it is midnight, allowing quiet for sleep, and the dog and all the different birds have fallen silent, a man who remembers the old ritual and fears the gods rises (his twin feet have no lacings) and forms a sign by joining his fingers with the middle of his thumb lest some slight ghost should meet him in the silence. And thrice he washes his hands pure in spring water; he turns, and puts black beans in his mouth. Turning aside he throws them away and doing so says 'These I release – with these beans I redeem me and mine.' Nine times he says this, without looking round. The ghost is thought to gather them and to follow behind (though no one sees it). Again he touches water, and he clashes Temesan cymbals, and he asks the ghost to leave his house. When he has said nine times, 'Leave, spirits of my fathers', he looks round and considers the rites performed with purity.
>
> OVID, *Fasti* 5.427-444

It is not just at the Lemuria that the dead are about: on three occasions during the year the *mundus*, a pit in the ground whose name also means 'universe', is ritually opened:

> 2.11 When the *mundus* is open, a sort of door is open for the mournful lower gods. For this reason, not only joining battle, but even recruiting for military service, setting out as a soldier, setting sail, marrying a wife in order to have children, are *religiosum* ['taboo'].
>
> VARRO, in Macrobius, *Saturnalia* 1.16.8

This oppressive character of Roman religion dominates the Roman calendar, where days were meticulously, legalistically distinguished with a letter or two to mark their *fas*-ness:

TYPES OF DAY IN THE ROMAN CALENDAR

Letter	No. days per year	Stands for	Meaning
N	57	*Nefasti*	Not *fas* for any non-religious business
NP	52	*Nefasti Publici*	*Nefas* because of major public festival
F	43	*Fasti*	Most activities are *fas*
C	192	*Comitiales*	Even public meetings are *fas*
EN	8	*Endotercisi* (i.e. *intercisi*)	'divided': early and late are *nefas*; mid-day is *fas*
QRCF	2	*Quando Rex Comitiavit Fas*	*Fas* after the king has held an assembly
QSDF	1	*Quando Stercus Delatum Fas*	*Fas* after the dung has been removed (annual cleaning of the temple of Vesta, 15 June)

I do not, however, believe that we have much understanding of the religious system implied by the Roman calendar (we understand the Athenian calendar better), because our evidence is so divorced from the time when the calendar was a living reality. Nor do we understand how a real society of men, women and children could find satisfaction in this system. Women, so prominently catered for in Greek religions, are conspicuous by their absence from the priesthoods and festivals of old Rome. Consequently, I am not going to discuss the old festivals any further. There is no point in amassing colourful detail, if sense cannot be made of it.

State and home

Making sense of the Penates
Public ceremony honoured big-name gods: these were the gods that Roman poets make so familiar, and in whom Romans found their own equivalents for the prestigious gods of the Greeks. Jupiter and Mars, Juno and Minerva, were of course 'the same as' Zeus and Ares, Hera and Athene. But they were not worshipped at home. So who was?

In Terence's *Phormio*, a comedy of 161 BC based on Greek plays, the old man Demipho returns after a long absence to a rather Roman-looking home:

2.12 'I'm going into the house to greet the *Di Penates*; then

I'm going on to the forum and I'll call up some of my friends
to help me in this business.'

TERENCE, *Phormio* 311-13

The *Di Penates* (*Penates*, for short) are the 'Gods of the Store-
Cupboard', though gods of the well-stocked freezer might be nearer
our modern ways of life. They were the heart of the home. You got in
touch with them at the hearth, which would be decorated with
garlands and receive offerings on the three main days of the month
(Kalends, Nones, and Ides – 1st, 7th/9th, 13th/15th respectively). This
has something of the rhythm of 'every Sunday'. But they would be
honoured every dinner-time too:

> 2.13 Amongst the Romans, when dinner had been served
> and the main course taken away, the custom was for there
> to be silence while an offering from the meal was taken to
> the hearth and put on the fire and a boy reported that the
> gods were propitious.
>
> SERVIUS, *Commentary on Vergil's Aeneid* 1.730

The Penates are meant here, but it can be seen that another god is
implied too: Vesta, the embodiment in goddess form of the hearth-
flame.

Greek religion has often been blamed for being unduly
'anthropomorphic', for thinking of gods too much in the shape of men.
Roman religion was less so: the Penates, Vesta and the Lares remain
rather shadowy and difficult to understand precisely because they
were not always thought of as persons. Varro could not say how many
Penates there were – they are just vaguely 'plural' – and it cannot be
ruled out that Vesta is in fact one of the *Di Penates*: 'all gods
worshipped at home are Penates' (Servius on *Aeneid* 2.514). They are
a distinctive Roman concept: Dionysios of Halikarnassos, explaining
them to his Greek audience (*Roman Antiquities* 1.67-68), tries five
different terms to describe them – none of which actually work.

Yet they are important enough to be represented at state level
too: in the *Aeneid* of Vergil (2.293-7, 3.11-12), Aeneas, who must
create the Roman identity out of the ashes of Troy, takes Vesta and
the Penates along with him. The oldest temple in Rome was supposed
to be that of the 'public Vesta of the Roman people, the *Quirites*'; she
had no statue, but had an inner and outer 'store-cupboard', *penus*,
the word from which Penates derives. The Penates had a little temple
of their own too, in which a sculptor, stumped for a Greek equivalent,
had desperately depicted them as 'two young men, seated and holding

spears', recollecting the Greek *Dioskouroi* (introduced to Rome as Castor and Pollux, chap. 3, p. 31); Vergil, on the other hand, borrowing a learned thought from the early historian Cassius Hemina, associates them with the 'Great Gods' (*Aeneid* 3.12), the mysterious cult of the *Kabeiroi* in Samothrace, which at least has the benefit of being as obscure as the Penates.

Home is where your Lar is
The *Lar* was, or at least had been, better defined. Plautus even begins a comedy with a Lar emerging from the home:

> 2.15 So no one wonders who I am, I'll tell you briefly: I am the *Lar Familiaris* of this *familia* here – where you saw me come out. I have owned and looked after this house for many years now – for the present occupier's father and grandfather before him. But it was his grandfather who entrusted to me treasure in gold – secretly from everyone: he buried it in the middle of the hearth, praying to me to look after it for him.
>
> PLAUTUS, *The Pot of Gold* 1-8

This Lar is a jovial spirit, protecting the family in its home from generation to generation. Here the householder prays to him to safeguard treasure, a special occasion; but he receives routine maintenance too, his monthly offering of incense.

So far he seems little different from the Penates (he could even *be* one of the Penates). But as *Lar familiaris* he looks after the whole *familia*, not just the 'family' in our sense but the whole population of the home and the land it is built on, including the slaves. After all, slaves too had a home, even if they did not own it, and this is recognised by their relationship with the Lar and their involvement in his worship – in particular in the *Compitalia* (or *Laralia*), a rural festival held early in January, in the quiet period of the year. It centred on points where several properties met, *compita*, or 'crossroads'. Here there would be a shrine to house the various Lares (also called a *compitum*), each facing his own property. A ploughshare would be hung up, and a wooden doll for each free person and a woollen ball for each slave: opposite, at the edge of each property, the *familia* would erect an altar at which to sacrifice. Why did slaves play so important a part in these ceremonies? We should think of those large properties in the country owned by great masters who were rarely present: in a real sense, these are the homes of the slaves, not of their masters and Cicero was even reluctant to be at his country house while his slaves were celebrating the *Compitalia* – 'in case I'm a nuisance to the *familia*' (*Letters to Atticus* 7.7.3).

This rural festival had unexpected repercussions on Roman politics. It was so valued that shrines to the Lares, *compita*, were set up at street corners in the city too, and the district officials, *(vico)magistri*, of local residents' associations, *collegia compitalicia*, arranged a *Compitalia* in which the main offering was cakes from each of the households. These were, however, associations of poor citizens, usually living in dismal blocks of flats, and could be turned to advantage by disruptive politicians. Associations of citizens outside the normal political framework were always viewed with suspicion, whether in the case of the *Bacchanalia* (chap. 3, pp. 37-9) or the Christians. The *collegia* were banned in 64 BC, were re-legalised by Clodius in 58 BC, banned again by Caesar and regulated by Augustus. Meanwhile lawyers debated how many made a *collegium*: perhaps three.

Before this political story continues we must add a new word: *Genius*. This denotes a special guardian spirit: places have protective spirits and so you may pray to the *Genius loci* ('Genius of the place') – even to the *Genius urbis Romae sive mas sive femina* ('Genius of the city of Rome whether male or female'). The snake represents the Genius in art. But a Genius can also be the guardian spirit of the *paterfamilias*, the formidable head of the family who originally had the authority of life and death over its members, only gradually restrained by concern for law and civilised values. On him depended the continuation of the family: hence the word *genius* is derived from 'beget' (*gen-*), and gives rise to 'marriage-bed' (*torus genialis*). Libations and sacrifices to the Genius were frequent, and an oath by the Genius of the *paterfamilias* would add special earnestness to what you had to say.

The political story of the Lares may now continue. Augustus (chap. 4, p. 60) reinforced his political control of Rome by allowing the *compitum* of the Lares to be the religious focus of each district, managed by four *magistri*: now there were two dancing youths, the *Lares praestites* ('guardian Lares'), in each – and a third object of worship, the *Genius Augusti*, the guardian spirit of the Emperor, depicted as a man sacrificing in his official toga. To swear falsely by this Genius could be viewed as treason.

The *Lares praestites* help bring the end for the singular Lar, though he was already drifting towards the plurality of the Penates.

Cult of the *Lares Augusti*, depicted on an altar set up by a *vicomagister*. Pig and sheep are ready for sacrifice, heads are covered and the pipes play.

In ancient houses, especially in Pompeii, we find free-standing mini-shrines (*aediculae*), gabled niches in the wall or niches painted on the wall. These are referred to in late Latin and by modern writers as *lararia*. In or on them appear two Lares, and a Genius of the *paterfamilias* depicted as a bearded and therefore male snake. Sometimes the Genius appears also as a man with head religiously covered by part of his toga, holding a *cornucopia* ('horn of plenty', overflowing with material wealth) or an incense-box in his right hand and with his left pouring a libation from a bowl: this is an idealisation of the *paterfamilias*. Sometimes, too, room could be found for other personally valued *objets*, particularly statuettes, of Fortune (with cornucopia, and rudder to steer your life), of Isis, or even (in Apuleius' novel) of the Gaulish goddess Epona – it all depended on what one considered important.

When paganism was finally banned, household cult was banned too. We catch our last glimpse of it in an edict of Theodosius dated 8 November AD 392, where it is stated that no one of any rank, high or low, shall:

> 2.15 in any place whatsoever, in any city, slay a harmless victim to statues that perceive nothing; nor shall he in a more private rite [*piaculum*], worship a Lar with fire, a Genius with neat wine, or Penates with fragrance, lighting fires, burning incense or hanging up garlands...
>
> If anyone worships statues, manufactured by man and subject to decay, by burning incense and presents an absurd specimen of immediate fear of his own fictions, by wreathing a tree with *vittae* [woollen streamers] or by digging turves and building an altar with them, trying to honour useless idols – even with a gift of humble value but nonetheless with utter wrongfulness as regards religion, then he shall on the charge of violating religion have the house or property confiscated on which he is proved to have been the servant of pagan religion.
>
> *Codex Theodosianus* 16.10.12

Chapter 3
The Controlled Republic

History begins with the end of the Kingdom – the rejection of Etruscan influence and the rise to world power of a city whose ruling aristocracy not only took over the political authority of the kings, but also kept a grip as firm as any king's over every detail of religion.

From the beginning of the Republic the aristocracy had a system for introducing new gods and rituals to maintain public morale at times of crisis. Does this give too cynical a picture? After all, the *sanctus Senatus* ('holy Senate'), whose members were the *patres conscripti* ('enrolled Fathers'), may have seen themselves as performing their duty as statesmen and guardians of tradition. To see them otherwise could be to impose the insincerity of our own world unjustly upon them.

All new introductions now came from Greek culture – the age of the Etruscans was over. But Greek culture did not just mean Greece: almost since the foundation of Rome, Greeks had lived in cities around the Italian and Sicilian coasts. Naples, for instance, is the Greek *Nea-polis* ('New Town'). So the tribes of Italy such as the Latins were in contact with Greek culture and religion from the earliest times. An early example was the Greek horsemen heroes Castor and Polydeuces (Latin, Pollux). They were popular in the Greek cities of southern Italy and had spread into the Italic cultures around Rome. Tradition tells that in a crucial moment of a cavalry battle in 499 BC a temple was vowed to these Greek heroes as an incentive to the troops:

> 3.1 At this point the dictator [Roman emergency leader] overlooked no aspect of divine or human assistance: he is said to have vowed a temple to Castor and to have advertised prizes for the first and second soldiers to enter the enemy camp.
>
> LIVY 2.20.12

This was duly built by 484 BC – to the joy of cavalry who paraded and sacrificed every 15 July, and was not without its part in humbler culture: women now swore by Castor, and men by Pollux – *mecastor! edepol!*

Reading the right books

Beginnings

But there was a more regular way to introduce new religions. This is
where the *IIviri Sacris Faciundis* ('Twomen for Conducting the Rites',
chap. 2, p. 16) come in. Their job was, when occasion demanded it,
i.e. when instructed by the Senate, to consult the Sibylline Books.
These books, written in Greek, were supposed to have been composed by a mythical prophetess of Apollo who lived at Cumae near
Naples, namely the Sibyl. The story went that she had sold only a few
of the books to King Tarquin the Ancient (Tarquinius Priscus) after
he had foolishly (being both a king and an Etruscan) refused to buy
them all. She burnt the rest. In these books, which only the IIviri could
consult, they always 'found' appropriate instructions for the introduction of Greek gods or practices – every one of their introductions
requiring the *ritus Graecus,* 'the Greek Rite' (so in these cases you
would *not* veil your head while sacrificing). The original books were
destroyed in a fire in 83 BC, though replacements were obtained by
76 BC and continued to be consulted until officially burnt shortly after
AD 400.

The first time the books were consulted, to our knowledge, was
in 496 BC. Problem: famine. Solution: Temple to Ceres, Liber and
Libera (really a Greek trio: Demeter the corn mother, Dionysus god
of wine, and Kore the daughter of Demeter). This temple, dedicated
in 493 BC, was the first (Varro said) to have a Greek rather than an
Etruscan cult statue. It became the centre of the Roman corn trade
and its importance for the lower classes may be judged by thinking
about who starves during famines.

From time to time the Board of the IIviri produced striking
innovations. A particular success was the introduction in 399 BC of
the *lectisternium,* to deal with plague, a recurring problem:

> 3.2 By decree of the Senate, the Sibylline Books were
> consulted. The *IIviri Sacris Faciundis* then for the first time
> in the city of Rome held a *lectisternium*: for eight days they
> placated Apollo and Latona, Hercules and Diana,
> Mercury and Neptune – with three couches (*lecti*) laid out
> (*strati*) as richly as could be prepared at that time.
>
> This rite was also celebrated by the general public.
> Throughout the city, doors were open and all manner of
> things were made freely available at the house fronts; every-
> where arrivals, known and unknown, were taken off and

treated to hospitality and kindly and affable conversation was held even with enemies. People refrained from quarrels and lawsuits. Even prisoners had their chains taken off for this period – and subsequently it was not felt right ['it was a *religio*', cf. chap. 1, p. 6] to enchain those to whom the gods had brought this assistance.

LIVY 5.13.5-8

Psychologically, this rare invitation of the gods to dinner in pairs, with its street-party sense of freedom and release, is beautifully judged. The *lectisternium* was a brilliant Roman development of the pleasing but routine annual West Greek original, the *Theodaisia* or *Theoxenia* – where the gods were invited to dine in person. There had been two repeat performances by 364 BC, and two more took place in 349 and 326.

Even rarer and more overwhelming was the Board's magnificent Tarentine Games, also known as the Centennial Games (*Ludi Saeculares*). In 249 BC the First Punic War was going badly and lightning had demolished part of the city wall, a portent designed to worry the superstitious. Rites of a hundred years earlier, including *lectisternium* and stage plays, were now declared an event which must happen every *saeculum*, a hundred years on most people's reckoning, renewing the original foundation of the city (in 753 BC or 751 BC or whenever). This was a once in a lifetime event – you would never see it again. But the rites were elaborated with dark, piacular elements. For three successive nights rites were conducted on the *Campus Martius*. These honoured the gods of the underworld, Dis and Proserpina, the victims were black, their altar (for the blood) was buried 20ft underground – at a mysterious point called 'Terentum' (hence the name 'Tarentine Games' by confusion with the name of the Greek city Tarentum).

The mathematics could be adjusted: the games come a little late in 146 BC; and Augustus, intent on renewing the city his own way, 'corrected' the method of calculation so that they might occur in 17 BC. They should have been held in the 40s BC: does Vergil envisage this in his fourth *Eclogue*, where he invokes the renewal of the age so vividly that Christians have sometimes thought he was predicting the birth of Christ? Is his imagination fired by the prospect of a renewal of the *saeculum* through the magnificent ceremony that the Xviri composed two hundred years before? In any case, the games continued according to *both* systems of reckoning until the last performance: by the Emperor Philip the Arab in AD 248.

Psychological war, with Hannibal
The Golden Era of the Sibylline Books was Rome's greatest and longest crisis, the Second Punic War, the war with Hannibal in which Rome suffered a series of agonising catastrophes. Even before the war, in 225 BC, the approach of the *Insubres* (a Celtic tribe) from the north caused panic in Rome and led to a rite of a barbarity which can alarm civilised modern Europeans...or ancient Greeks:

> 3.3 The Romans do not have any barbaric or outlandish practices. In fact, their ways of thought are, as much as any could be, of a Greek character and mild towards matters divine. But then, as the war fell upon them, they were compelled to give way to oracles in the Sibylline Books and bury alive two Greeks, man and woman, and two Gauls similarly, in the *Forum Boarium* [Ox-Market]. And still, in the month of November they perform secret, hidden rites to them.
> PLUTARCH, *Biography of Marcellus* 3

A repeat of this atrocious rite 'in accordance with the Books of Fate' in 216 BC after the Battle of Cannae, Rome's worst ever defeat, elicits the comment from Livy that human sacrifice was a 'thoroughly un-Roman rite' (*minime Romano sacro*, 22.57.6). Those with uneasy stomachs may regard the repeat of the story at a different date as suspicious and view it as one of those myths that 'explains' a ritual (an *aetiological* myth). Personally, I am not so sure: there was indeed a decree of the Senate banning human sacrifice – but it was passed in 97 BC (Pliny *HN* 30.12).

Less doubt surrounds the extravagant range of rites which the Board designed to placate and appease the shattered minds and emotions of the Roman people after the disastrous defeat at Lake Trasimene the previous year, when it was thought that Hannibal might descend upon Rome at any instant:

> 3.4 Quintus Fabius Maximus, serving his second term as dictator, on the first day of his magistracy called the Senate and began with the gods. The mistake of Gaius Flaminius the consul, he informed the Fathers [Senate], lay more in his neglect of the ceremonies and auspices than in haste and ignorance. To find out the correct *piacula* for the gods' anger [*ira deorum*], the gods themselves should be consulted. His motion was passed – a rare one except when appalling prodigies are reported – that the Xviri should be instructed to consult the Sibylline Books. On inspecting these Books of Fate, they reported to the Fathers that

* with respect to the vow made to Mars on account of that war, it had not been correctly performed and needed to be done all over again and on a larger scale;
* they should vow Great Games to Jupiter and a temple to Venus of Eryx [in Sicily, see *Aeneid* 5.759-60] and *Mens* ['Mind/Purpose'];
* they should hold a *supplicatio* and a *lectisternium*;
* they should vow a *ver sacrum*, to be held if the war turned out as they hoped and the state remained in the same condition as before the war.

LIVY 22.9.7-10

A worried public is assured that failure in war is the result simply of insufficient piety: they are experiencing not simply military defeat, but the *ira deorum* when they need the *pax deorum*. Rites that have to be performed again undo the old disasters and distract the mind. Games energise the community and restore mutual confidence. The *Supplicationes* were powerful ritual tours of shrine after shrine by the whole population: they developed into a close companion to the *lectisternium*, in which the various 'couches' of the gods would be toured, and served to increase the intensity of the *lectisternium*. Mightiest of all, though, is the Board's remarkable reinterpretation of the ancient Italian custom of the Sacred Spring (*ver sacrum*). In its original form, the young (i.e. new adults) of a community would be dedicated to a god and sent off to find a new home and (more to the point) new land elsewhere. But in this revamped version, all the animals born that spring – piglets, lambs, kids and calves – are to be given up, to be sacrificed (in the Roman sense and in ours) to the gods. What more could the gods want?

A useful tool
Intelligent Greeks were often struck by the Romans' scrupulous attention to religion. Dionysios of Halikarnassos is overwhelmed: he even believes the claim that their devotion to religion accounts for their success in war:

> 3.5...so that for those who do not know the piety which the Romans practised in those times it may not seem surprising that all their wars ended so well. For you will see that they conducted the beginnings and basics of all of them with immense piety and for this reason in particular had the gods on their side in times of danger.

DIONYSIOS OF HALIKARNASSOS, *Roman Antiquities* 2.72.3

Others took a more detached, cynical and unscrupulously Greek view. Notably the statesman and historian Polybios, who spent much of his life at Rome:

> 3.6 The Roman constitution seems to me to have the greatest difference for the better in its policy on religion. Indeed I think that something one would criticise in the case of other peoples in fact holds the Roman state together, namely its superstition. This aspect is infiltrated with such theatricality amongst them, both in their private lives and in the city's public affairs, that it is impossible to exaggerate – which might seem strange to many. Yet for my part I think they have done this because of the masses, because if it were possible to assemble a state out of intelligent men, perhaps there would be no necessity for this sort of thing; but since the masses are always unthinking and full of lawless desires, irrational passion, and violent spirits, one can only keep the masses under control by obscure fears and this sort of theatricality.
>
> POLYBIOS 6.56.6-11

Towards the end of the Second Punic War, in 204 BC, the Books demanded the introduction of the cult of Cybele, the *Magna Mater* ('Great Mother'), together with colourful rites and entertaining games, the *Megale(n)sia*. The cult came from Pergamum, one of Rome's more distant allies, otherwise of little interest to a war-weary population. But by now the great age of the Sibylline Books was drawing to a close and the inspiration with which they had been 'consulted' drained away. It is true that even the Emperors continued to consult the Books when a traditional, secure and proper approach to religion made good publicity, but there is little new to report. Look finally at this, after the great fire of Rome under Nero in AD 66:

> 3.7 Presently, the gods were asked about *piacula* and the Sibylline Books were consulted, in accordance with which there was a *supplicatio* for Volcanus [god of fire], and Ceres and Proserpina; and Juno was propitiated by the married women, first on the Capitol Hill, then at the sea's nearest point – from there they drew water and sprinkled the temple and the goddess's statue with it; and there were *sellisternia* [like *lectisternia*, but with seats instead of couches] and vigils celebrated by women with living husbands.
>
> TACITUS, *Annals* 15.44

How much ice did this cut in a more sophisticated age, a quarter of a millennium after the end of the Second Punic War? Tacitus certainly implies it was not enough and alleges that Nero then tapped a different source of emotional satisfaction: persecuting the Christians – who in their own way disturbed the *pax deorum* (chap. 6, pp. 80-1).

Non-approved cults

With control of religious innovation went suppression of the innovations of others. This can tell us much about the religious assumptions of the aristocracy, as a few early examples will show.

The Bacchanalia

This inscription was set up in 186 BC:

> 3.8 Quintus Marcius son of Lucius, and Spurius Postumius son of Lucius, consuls, held a meeting of the Senate on the Nones of October at the temple of Bellona. Present at the writing down were Marcus Claudius son of Marcus, Lucius Valerius son of Publius, and Quintus Minucius son of Gaius.
>
> Concerning the *Bacchanales* [worshippers of Bacchus] who are of Allied Status, they decided on the following proclamation:
> * That none of them should wish to hold a Bacchanal; or if there are any who claim it is necessary for them to hold a Bacchanal, that they should come to the Urban Praetor and that after a hearing our Senate should decide about these matters, provided that not less than 100 Senators be present when this matter is discussed.
> * That no man should wish to approach the Bacchae [female worshippers], neither Roman Citizen, nor anyone of Latin or Allied Status, except if they have approached the Urban Praetor and he has given permission in accordance with the opinion of the Senate provided that not less than 100 Senators be present when this matter is discussed. Decided.
> * That no man should be a priest, nor any man or woman be a president. And that none of them should wish to hold common funds, nor anyone wish to appoint either man or woman to a magistracy or promagistracy. And that they should not afterwards wish to make between them joint

oaths, vows, promises, or undertakings; and that no one should wish to create a bond of loyalty between them.

* And that no one should wish to perform rites in secret, nor anyone to perform rites in public or in private or outside the city, unless he has approached the Urban Praetor [...etc. etc.]

* That not more than a total of 5 men and women should wish to perform rites, nor that on such occasion should more than 2 men or more than 3 women wish to attend, except in accordance with the opinion of the Urban Praetor and the Senate, as written above.

* ...[rules for display of the decree]...if anyone contravenes what is written above, they have decided it is to be considered a capital offence...

INSCRIPTION, *CIL* 1^2.581

Not Roman. The limp god Dionysus with pet panther and other indignified companions.

Bacchus is the name applied to the Greek god Dionysos when he is associated with uninhibited forms of cult, where dancing and alcohol brought release from the concerns of routine life. But these rites, which spread easily through Greece and through the Greek cities of Italy, were also secret – you had to undergo special, initiatory rites before you could take part. In these regulations we see a determined effort to eliminate the organisation of the cult: no officers are to be allowed and no groups are to gather (compare worries about *collegia* chap. 2, pp. 26-7). The cult is viewed as socially disruptive and sexually immoral. Livy has a long and memorable account of the suppression of this cult revealing without sympathy how brutally it was stamped out:

> 3.9 More were killed than thrown into chains – and there was a great number in both categories – men and women. Condemned women were handed over to their relatives or guardians so that they might deal with them in private; if there was no suitable person to exact the punishment, they were dealt with publicly. Then the consuls were given the task of demolishing all Bacchic cult places – at Rome first, then throughout Italy – apart from if they found some ancient altar or statue consecrated there.
>
> LIVY 39.18.5-7

You should have no doubt what was done to the women: they were executed. And there was no support in the tabloids: no-one appealed to the People and no tribune intervened to help. But the god is not dishonoured: legal provision has been made for genuine devotion (though of course there isn't any) and no genuinely religious altar or statue is destroyed. You can tell it's genuine because it's old. New is fake, impious, immoral. (The Xviri introduced nothing new – it was all in the ancient Sibylline Books, wasn't it?)

Excesses in the name of Cybele
The cult of Cybele, introduced by the Xviri at the end of the Second Punic War (above, p. 36), was sanitised. Nothing wild or frenzied was to reach Roman citizens or slaves – official religion, new or old, is for spectators only. Dionysios of Halikarnassos, explaining Roman customs to Greeks around 7 BC, has praise for this:

> 3.10 What I admire above all is that although thousands of foreign nationalities have come to the city and they naturally must worship their ancestral gods in accordance

with practices at home, the City has not publicly developed
enthusiasm for any foreign practices – something which has
happened in many cities before now – and even if it has
introduced some rites in accordance with oracles [i.e.
Sibylline Books], they worship them with their own
procedure, rejecting all mythological claptrap, as in the
case of the rites of the Idaean Mother [Cybele]. Here the
magistrates celebrate sacrifices and games to her every
year according to Roman customs; but her priesthood goes
to a Phrygian man and a Phrygian woman, and it is these
who do the rounds of the city Mother-begging [collecting
for the Great Mother, Cybele], as their custom is, with
medallions on their chests and they have Mother-songs
played at them on the flute by those following them and
they beat tambourines. No native Roman either goes
Mother-begging or has the flute played at him through the
city, wearing gaudy clothes, or worships the goddess with
the Phrygian rites – by law and decree of the Senate.
DIONYSIOS OF HALIKARNASSOS, *Roman Antiquities* 2.19

There were worse things than wearing gaudy clothes. The Cybele cult
was noted for a particularly unpleasant excess of enthusiasm, vividly
portrayed in Catullus' 63rd poem: self-castration (with stone-age
flint). Such instances were bluntly dealt with. In 101 BC 'a slave of
Servilius Caepio chopped himself in honour of the Idaean Mother and
was transported overseas never to return to Rome' (Livy 68, fr. in
Julius Obsequens). And in 77 BC one Genucius, who had similarly
mutilated himself, was involved in a legal case over property; but the
consul Aemilius Mamercus denounced him as neither a man nor a
woman and decreed that 'the obscene presence and befouled voice
of Genucius should not, under the pretext of seeking justice, pollute
the tribunals of magistrates'! (VALERIUS MAXIMUS, *Famous Words
and Deeds* 7.7.6).

Isis

The Roman establishment had only itself to blame for having let loose
the religion of Cybele, but the 'Egyptian' gods (chap. 5, pp. 66-74)
were introduced against its will by lower classes. A rather muddled
inscription seemingly from before 58 BC presents us with the names
of freedmen and freedwomen responsible for the cult of Isis on the
Capitol Hill. Their 'temple', probably a humble construction, was
repeatedly the subject of demolition orders from the Senate, but was

equally repeatedly rebuilt. Feelings ran high. In 58 BC the crowds prevented the consul Gabinius from taking the auspices as he entered on his consulship 'because he had made no decision about Serapis and Isis' (Varro, fr. 46). With aristocratic disdain, he 'considered the Senate's judgment more important than the impulse of the mob and forbade the altars to be set up'.

There was a repeat showing in 50 BC:

> 3.11 When the Senate had decreed that the shrines of Isis and Serapis should be destroyed and none of the workmen dared to touch them, the consul Aemilius Paulus took off his official robe, picked up an axe and struck the doors of that temple.
>
> VALERIUS MAXIMUS, *Famous Words and Deeds* 1.3.4

This situation continued into the 40s BC but looked like coming to an end when in 43 BC the triumvirs (Mark Antony, Octavian – the later Augustus – and Lepidus) voted a temple to Serapis and Isis. However, the return of civil war and Antony's joining forces with Cleopatra of Egypt put the Egyptian gods back on the losing side. Vergil describes the scene at the decisive battle, Actium (31 BC), in Octavian's colours:

> 3.12 The queen in the midst calls forth the columns with ancestral rattle [the *sistrum* – a typical bit of Isis gear]. Nor does she yet see behind her twin snakes [referring to her death]. And monstrous gods of every kind and barker Anubis [he has a jackal's head] against Neptune and Venus and against Minerva [good Romans all] hold their weapons.
>
> VERGIL, *Aeneid* 8.696-700

The cult of the Egyptian gods was kept beyond the sacred city limits of Rome [the *pomerium*] under both Augustus and Tiberius. Only under Gaius 'Caligula' (Emperor AD 37-41), who admired Egyptian customs to the extent of sleeping with his sister, was the cult incorporated into the official calendar. But horizons have narrowed since the *Bacchanalia*: in this case we see the Senate acting not so much as the government of an empire, but as the city council of Rome – repeatedly refusing planning permission and protecting the city's culture. Beyond Rome, for instance in Pompeii, you might win friends and influence people by belonging to the Isis cult.

Endgame: 63-48 BC

In this section I take a look at some telling moments in the politico-religious life of the late Republic.

Caesar for Pontifex Maximus!

In the 60s BC, Julius Caesar had not yet reached the heights of power we associate with his name. The military campaigns in Gaul (58-49 BC) were still to come. And he was still to reach his first consulship, of 59 BC. This was the situation when in 63 BC the post of Pontifex Maximus, the highest ranking priesthood in Rome, fell free. We might imagine now that religious authorities would be consulted about the most appropriate man to appoint to the post; and we can easily imagine the sort of qualities that the ideal appointee might possess: perhaps a pious way of life, or an astonishing command of ritual and tradition. But no, this was a political honour, fought viciously between the politicians who already were *pontifices*, and on which the people voted. The only concession to religion was the quaint practice, recently reintroduced, that the Pontifex Maximus was appointed by vote of only 17 of the 35 tribes – a minority (selected by lot).

So desperate was the distinguished politician Catulus that he offered an enormous bribe to Caesar (a mere 37-year-old) to stand down. Caesar did not, and his growing control of political support narrowly ensured his success. Caesar has sometimes been thought an Epicurean (who believed the gods did not bother themselves about man, whose rituals were a waste of time, except inasmuch as they were enjoyable and sociable). According to Suetonius 'He was never deterred from any course of action, or even delayed, by any religious considerations' (*Life of the Divus Julius* 59). This was the man who would now be in charge of the state's rituals. It was no different fifteen years later: just before Caesar defeated Pompey at the Battle of Pharsalus (48 BC) and settled the fate of the Roman world, Caesar tells us that there was 'daily wrangling' in the Pompeian camp about who would succeed Caesar as Pontifex Maximus (*Civil War* 3.83).

Sky-watching

Caesar became consul in 59 BC and set about a legislative programme to which his fellow-consul, Bibulus, was bitterly opposed. Normally this would have produced stalemate, but Caesar and his supporters resorted to violence to keep Bibulus away from the assembly that passed his laws. Desperately, Bibulus played one last card: religion.

He announced from his mansion that he intended to watch the heavens on any day when Caesar tried to pass a law. As a bemused Dio remarks (38.13), in these cases it did not matter whether he saw anything, good sign or bad; it was enough simply to watch the heavens in order to prevent meetings of the assembly from taking place legitimately. Of course, they just took place illegitimately instead, but the very fact that Bibulus thought such a ploy worthwhile and not wholly absurd means that there was still some religious force in it in his day, however little.

In the following year, 58 BC, Cicero's bitter enemy Clodius, an energetic and popular figure with no time for the Bibuluses of this world, took Bibulus' religious ploy seriously enough to pass a law:

> 3.13 that no magistrate should, on the days on which it was necessary for the People to vote on any matter, look for signs from the heavens.
>
> CASSIUS DIO 38.13

These were the games politicians were playing while the lowest classes struggled to establish their cult of Isis (above, pp. 40-1), unhelped by any politician however 'popular'.

Cicero and the place for religion

Presently, Clodius forced Cicero into exile. Cicero's letter to his wife as he reaches Brindisi on 29 April 58 BC casts a strange light on Cicero's attitude to religion:

> 3.14...neither the gods you have always so purely worshipped nor the men to whom I have always given service have been grateful.
>
> CICERO, *Letters to his Friends* 14.4.1

In fact, there are parts of Cicero's writings which give the impression that he thought traditional religion good for the maintenance of law and order, though it gave a false picture of the gods; this, however, 'should not be discussed in public, as such discussion might destroy the established religion' (CICERO, *On the Nature of the Gods*, fragment in Lactantius, *Divine Institutes* 2.3.2). Indeed, when he distinguishes between religion and superstition, it is only his love of tradition that saves him from branding Roman religion as superstition:

> 3.15 But I want it distinctly understood that the destruction of superstition does not mean the destruction of religion.

> For I consider it the function of wisdom to preserve the
> institutions of our forefathers, by retaining their sacred
> rites and ceremonies. Furthermore, the celestial order and
> the beauty of the universe compel me to confess that there
> is some excellent and eternal being who deserves the
> respect and homage of men.
>
> CICERO, *On Divination* 2.148-9

This 'excellent and eternal being' undoubtedly lives in the pages of
Greek philosophers and would have been wholly unknown to Cicero's
simpler, Roman forefathers with all their 'sacred rites and ceremonies'.

The end is nigh

So in this period, amongst the elite of Rome, there were several
degrees of belief in the value and effectiveness of traditional religion,
though mostly low on the scale. Yet religion and superstition were
controversial issues of the day, perhaps encouraged by the perception
of a political system in a state of terminal decay, with violence on the
streets and a whole mood of instability. This was when Varro and
Nigidius Figulus were writing (chap. 2, pp. 14-16). And it is no
coincidence that Lucretius, a man of the same age as Julius Caesar,
but who died around 55 or 53 BC, left us his great poem on
Epicureanism denouncing superstition, at much the same time as the
tribune Ateius Capito, having exhausted all legal avenues for
restraining Crassus from setting out to attack Parthia, finally, in
desperation, met him as he departed at the gates of Rome:

> 3.16...he burnt incense and poured libations and called
> down curses upon him – terrible and horrifying curses,
> invoking by name amidst them fearful and weird gods. The
> Romans say these curses, ancient and mysterious, have
> such power that no one bound by them can escape and that
> even he who uses them fares ill.
>
> PLUTARCH, *Life of Crassus* 16

The curses worked: Crassus was disastrously defeated and slaughtered at the Battle of Carrhae (53 BC); and Capito's political career
was at an end – the establishment saw to it.

A son of Crassus was also killed at Carrhae. He was an augur.
Cicero was proud to succeed to this position (if rather late in life for
this post, usually given to the sons of the elite), though it disconcerts
both St Augustine and ourselves that in his work *On Divination*,
Cicero demonstrates that divination (including augury) cannot work.

Chapter 4
Empire and Provinces

Government policy: tolerance

Unlike modern governments, the government of Rome rarely intervened in anything unless it had to. Nowhere is this more true than in religion. Only perhaps in the case of the cult of the emperor himself did the Roman centre devise a policy for the provinces – and that was aided and abetted by its subjects. For the most part emperors did not impose an official religion and probably could not. Nor would they wish to interfere with the established religions of their subjects. Persecution of the Christians was different, as strictly they were defectors from the religion of their ancestors (see chap. 6, p. 88). Even so, persecutions were largely the product of local demands before the edict of Decius in AD 249: the execution of Jesus is itself typical – this was the governor Pontius Pilatus placating local worthies.

In the provinces central government was represented by the governor. And theoretically the powers delegated to him were as great as communications were poor. Yet they were limited too: he might not rashly commit armies to battle, he needed to be able to give an accurate account of his financial administration, and above all his job was to react to provincial demands in such a way as to minimise trouble. The delicacy of this task can be seen in an incident from the correspondence of Pliny with the Emperor Trajan. The people of Nicomedia are building a new Forum and wish to re-site the temple of the *Magna Mater*; Pliny, as governor, has checked the propriety according to Roman law of so moving the temple, but first clears it with Trajan, who replies:

> 4.1 You may, my very dear Pliny, move the temple of the Mother of the Gods without any worries about religious propriety to the more suitable position, if that is what the location seems to demand. Do not be concerned at finding no Rule of Dedication, as the ground of a foreign state does not admit dedication according to our law.
>
> TRAJAN in PLINY, *Letters* 10.50

Behind the last sentence can be seen a respect for local religious customs and an unwillingness to challenge them. And this was the rule for the whole Empire, that local religious practices continued undisturbed where they represented the heritage of a nation. This is a matter both of convenience for the rulers of an empire (the Persians had done the same) and of the in-built tolerance of paganism, in which conversion (except from the barbarity of human sacrifice) was unnecessary: the gods made room for more or appeared locally in different guises. This is a policy which only comes to an end with the intolerance of later, Christian emperors (chap. 6, pp. 89-90).

'Paganism'

The religious freedom of the Roman Empire resulted in a large number of religions. Not in the sense that inhabitants of the empire would be choosing daily between religions, but in the sense that the mosaic of local traditions continued undisturbed. These local traditions, rather than the (international) official or exotic cults, were what religion meant to the overwhelming majority of the Empire's inhabitants until Christianity made significant headway (e.g., by around AD 400 in Gaul).

When we use the word 'paganism', we refer to all these non-Christian traditions. *Paganus* (strictly, a 'villager') seems to have become slang for an 'ordinary person', someone who had not signed up – for Christianity. *Paganitas* and *paganismus* are Christian terms ('outsiderdom') already in use by the time of Augustine (c. AD 400). But they can mislead us: 'paganism' implies no system – there never was such a thing as a 'paganist'. From the point of view of Christianity pagans had much in common: many gods (*polytheism*), worship of statues (*idolatry*) and sacrifices. But that just shows how different Christianity was. For most of the world, religion consisted of sacrifice, festivals and shrines of gods who with their various names and functions more or less systematically covered the needs of their communities. As civilization reached the shrines of the remoter provinces, finally temples would be built. Only barbarians like the Scythians and the Germans had no temples.

The interpretatio Romana

Pagans did, however, respond to the arrival of Rome and adopt a limited uniformity into their local systems – by presenting local gods as Roman gods under another name. So, for instance, in Britain we find inscriptions to the British gods Maponus and Cocidius, but also to Apollo Maponus and Mars Cocidius, where Apollo and Mars are the supposed Roman equivalents, the *interpretatio Romana*. Often the local name is omitted: inscriptions to Deus Mars ('the god Mars'), more rarely just 'Mars', make it quite unclear which god we are really talking about.

This is not helped by the official, formal nature of inscriptions, which demands Latin: none at all are written in British (i.e. Brythonic, the ancestor of Welsh), though a handful are written in Gaulish, as we shall see. Latin inscriptions tend to be about Latin gods – the *interpretatio Romana* of local gods and goddesses. So 'Mercury' is extremely popular in Gaul, because his name is applied to various local gods. Of course the local gods must resemble Mercury in some way to be identified with him. But only 'in some way': it does not give us more than the broadest outline. What did an ancient Gaul think the Roman Mercury was like? (Look at p. 51.)

Interpretatio Romana is a feature of the Western provinces. In the East, the question had long been how to respond to Greek culture, which takes us beyond the bounds of this book. In the West, the provinces were rather underdeveloped except where colonies, i.e. model Roman cities, had been planted. People in the Western provinces measured their importance in urbanisation, Romanisation. To set up a Latin inscription is a way, maybe quite an expensive way, of taking part in this process. And it will of course be unrepresentative of most of the population, notably rural peasants. Ordinary people just got on with their local religion and pass, ignored, out of history.

Local cults

Local religions varied greatly and are profoundly ignored in our main sources of evidence – literary texts and inscriptions. However, it may help to consider Gaul, a crossroads of native culture, Romanisation and Christianisation. And the evidence is perhaps a little fuller there than in Britain. I then add some notes on Britain, where it is particularly difficult to put together a coherent picture, and on Greece, where – by contrast – it is particularly easy. Ideally one should look at every province, but these will make a useful start.

Gaul

Gaul is where Gauls lived. That even included northern Italy (for instance Milan and Bologna), which was known as *Gallia Cisalpina*

('Gaul on this side of the Alps'), so assimilated by Roman Italy that in 49 BC all its inhabitants became Roman citizens. On the other side of the Alps, the south of France had become a Roman province very early (125-118 BC) – hence its modern name, 'Provence' – and was thoroughly Romanised. Narbonne was a colony of Roman citizens sent out in 118 BC. And by the time of Pliny the province could be regarded as 'Italy more than a province' (Pliny *HN* 3.31). So far we are in *Gallia togata* ('Gaul that wears the toga'). The vast area to the north, *Gallia comata* ('long-haired Gaul'), was brought under Roman control by Caesar in 58-51 BC and formed three provinces (the 'Three Gauls'), namely Lugdunensis (including Lyon – Lugdunum – and Paris), Aquitania (including Bordeaux) and Belgica (including Reims and Trier).

Romanisation, then, had a firm hold in the South even before the annexations of Caesar and it obviously succeeded in the end, as the domination of French, the descendant of Latin, shows. Celtic language now survives only in Brittany, and derives (at least for the most part) from Cornish-speaking immigrants in the fifth century AD. Together with Romanisation also goes the early and relatively complete success of Christianity in France, assured by around AD 400. But what religion were the numerous inhabitants of the Gauls practising until then? Here problems of evidence begin.

It is remarkable that there are any inscriptions actually written in Gaulish. They are very few, written in Greek letters, and may be narrowly pre-Roman. Here is one, together with rather a guess-work translation:

4.2	SEGOMAROS	Segomaros
	WILLONEOS	Willoneos (i.e. son of Will- ?)
	TOOUTIOUS	of the people
	NAMAUSATIS	of Nemausa (Nîmes)
	EIOROUBELE	made for Belesamis (*int. rom.*: Minerva)
	SAMISOSIN	this
	NEMETON	grove/sanctuary

INSCRIPTION, *CIL* XII 162

An isolated inscription cannot tell us much. This one tells us that Celts too have the practice of marking out sacred precincts to their own gods (no great surprise). No temple is mentioned: stone temples have maybe not yet reached Gaulish culture. What inscriptions should matter for, though even this can be treacherous, is statistics: one can see the relative popularity of gods, their distribution, gain some view of the attitudes of representative samples of worshippers. The Gaulish inscriptions are too few to make a sample.

So what of Gaulish writers? To be a writer one would use Latin and subscribe to Roman values. There is no literature in Gaulish. And no Gauls writing in Latin (of which there are few enough anyway) chose to blot their civilized copy-book by describing native religion. The nearest we get is Ausonius' little set of poems in praise of the 'Professors of Bordeaux' of the AD 380s:

> 4.3 Nor shall I pass over the old man Phoebicius [a professor]; he was the temple-keeper of Belenus [Gaulish god = Apollo] but got no help from that; however, born – as is agreed – of Druid stock, of the race of Aremorica, he got the chair [of rhetoric] at Bordeaux by his son's efforts.
>
> AUSONIUS, *Remembering the Professors of Bordeaux* 10.22-30

So in the late fourth century, Celtic gods and 'Druid stock' were something you could be proud of. But they look folksy and Ar(e)morica is remote Brittany.

Latin and Greek writers? They scarcely spare a moment for Gaulish religion and when they do they are rather obsessed with Druids and human sacrifice. Even Caesar begins his brief account of Gaulish religion with the remark 'The whole nation of the Gauls is much given to religious practices' – and continues with the prevalence (as he thinks) of human sacrifice, under Druidic management (*Gallic War* 6.16.1).

Druids are special to Gaul and Britain. They are an inherited priestly class (ultimately corresponding to Indian brahmans and the rather worn-out Roman *flamines*). They are also very upper-class. Their association with human sacrifice gave the Roman regime a public reason for eliminating them, though one may suspect that they got in the way of efficient Roman control of Gallic society. In particular they had strong links with Britain and it was surely as he invaded Britain that the Emperor Claudius took the final step:

> 4.4 The religion of the Druids amongst the Gauls, one of terrible savagery and only forbidden to Roman citizens by Augustus, was completely abolished.
>
> SUETONIUS, *Life of Claudius* 25

This would certainly have some impact on Gaulish religion, though modern writers do tend to exaggerate this point.

We know that there had been a Gaulish mythology, but we do not know what it contained – except that 'the Gauls say they are all sprung from father Dis and that this has been handed down by the Druids'. (CAESAR, *Gallic War* 6.18). Dis is for Romans the under-world god, and this myth looks as though it continues a particular Indo-European myth reflected distantly in Indian mythology (Yama, king of the dead) and, much transmuted, in the Roman myth of Romulus and Remus. Otherwise, the oral (i.e. word-of-mouth) tradition died out without trace: the suppression of the Druids, responsible for 'education' and passing on tradition, must have taken its toll. One other detail impressed classical writers about the Druids: their apparently sophisticated doctrine of the immortality of the human soul. But it is only a corollary of the not very sophisticated practice of including the goods of this life in burials for use in the next.

Having got Druids off his chest, Caesar goes on to a brief description of the Gaulish system of gods – though heavily infected by *interpretatio Romana*:

> 4.5 Their most important god is Mercury. His are most statues; him they claim as discoverer of all skills; him they consider their leader in journeys and travel, and he they think has most power over money-making and trade. Second come Apollo, Mars, Jupiter and Minerva. About them they have much the same ideas as other peoples: Apollo eliminates diseases, Minerva passes on basic crafts and techniques, Jupiter holds power over the gods of heaven, Mars governs war.
>
> CAESAR, *Gallic War* 6.17.1-2

These are the 'long-haired' Gauls at the moment when they are drawn into the Roman sphere. Gradually their hair will be shorter, they will sprout togas, speak Latin and have less use for a war-god, whatever name is hidden under 'Mars'. But trade and travel, the domain of 'Mercury', will become more important to the inscription-writing classes.

Three awesome sanctuaries on mountain peaks (Puy-de-Dôme, Donon, Châtelard-de-Lardiers) have been associated with 'Mercury' – rather out of the reach of travellers and tradesmen, one would have thought. The difficulty in making these sanctuaries and the god fit with our notions of Roman religion at least shows the extent to which native religion survived in a distinctive form and indeed benefited from the introduction of new technology and prosperity. Two further large

Is this Mercury? The hat is right, but an inscription tells us that this is the
Gaulish Esus.

sanctuaries (Sanxay and Grand) have been tied to 'Apollo'. Grand is particularly interesting: wealthy enough to have the largest figured mosaic in Europe, and also a centre for healing – perhaps by *incubation* (sleeping in the sanctuary and having the god appear in a dream to deliver instructions). The name 'Grand' comes from the real name of the god – 'Grannus', a god particularly of spas and healing waters, who can be found from Sweden to Germany (Aachen, Wiesbaden), consulted by Caracalla, and found in Scotland too:

4.6

TO APOLLO GRANNUS
QUINTUS LUSIUS SABINIANUS IMPERIAL PROCURATOR
V.S.L.M.*   * (see p. 5)
INSCRIPTION from Inveresk (8 km E. of Edinburgh), *RIB* 2132

This is no Briton. He is a figure of some authority, a senior civil servant posted to Britain and understandably falling ill. He prays to a native god (which shows that Romans could believe sufficiently in the gods of other provinces). He recovers and thankfully leaves this *ex voto*.

Awesome sanctuaries are the tip of a humbler iceberg, as St Martin (Bishop of Tours AD 372-97) found when he went around ruthlessly and intolerantly destroying shrine after pagan shrine and reducing 'all altars and statues to dust':

> 4.7 When in a certain village he had demolished a temple of great antiquity and had set about chopping down a pine tree next to the shrine, at that point the priest of that place and the rest of the pagans began to obstruct him. And though these same had, at the Lord's command, remained quiet while the temple was destroyed, they would not allow the tree to be chopped down. St Martin carefully pointed out to them that there is nothing religious about a tree-stump.
>
> SULPICIUS SEVERUS, *Life of St Martin* 13

Real Gaulish religion may have had a nature-look. Here we see trees, but springs too were a focus of religious attention, which Christianity had to divert. The crypt of Chartres cathedral, for instance, is sited at one.

Festivals obviously figured in Gaulish religion. In the time of St Martin, 'this was the custom of Gaulish peasants, to carry statues of demons [i.e. pagan gods] covered in white veiling around their fields out of their wretched idiocy' (SULPICIUS SEVERUS, *Life of St Martin* 12). Such local devotion had to be defused by the Christians. At

Brioude (Auvergne), a festival of 'Mercury' and 'Mars' in the earlier fifth century gave way to a festival of St Julian at some time before AD 469. There was also a flurry of introductions of local cults of saints in the later fifth century, surely replacing local paganism. Certainly a story associated St Julian's newly-severed head with a nearby health-restoring spring: that has the look of an earlier, more gruesome age. Local religion was a continuing need. Christianity did not just obliterate paganism – it occupied its physical and mental space.

Britain in brief

Britain was taken into the Roman Empire under Claudius, beginning in AD 43. Britons, like Gauls, were Celts, and some belonged to the same tribes. There must therefore have been significant similarities in religion, and indeed several of the same gods were worshipped. But Britain was not a clone of Gaul (and doubtless Gaulish religion was not uniform either): Celtic religion varied from place to place, as most paganisms do.

Britain was a backward place, with no tradition of towns and only a rudimentary participation in trade. Colonies (model towns) were established gradually (e.g. Colchester, Lincoln, York) and in the end a level of prosperity was reached. Nonetheless, I cannot think of a single pagan British writer during the whole Roman Empire; and Christian British authors only amount to the heretic Pelagius (died AD 416) and his follower Fastidius (bishop around AD 430). Even the official cults made slow progress (below, p. 63-4). Latin – or urban life – was not sufficiently deeply rooted when Roman power receded: the speech of Britain in the Roman Empire is represented by Welsh, Breton and Cornish – Celtic languages all.

There are no inscriptions in the native language – and much of the inscriptional activity belongs to the military zone. Nevertheless, a careful look at the scanty remains gives us a glimpse of:

* Sacred groves and the power of springs and wells. In some places there was a progression from a natural site of religion to the erection of a temple, maybe first in wood and later in stone. The increasing prosperity of Britain in the later Empire allowed more building of stone temples (in distinctive 'Romano-British' shapes), which can give a misleading impression of a 'pagan revival' in the third/fourth centuries AD.

* An unhealthy interest in skulls: 14 were found in a pool at

Wookey Hole in Somerset, apparently dating from the Roman Empire – and aged mainly between 25 and 30. Celtic legends associate severed heads with wells and pools (cf. St Julian's head, above, p. 53).

* The most frequent Roman god-name (usually thanks to *int. Rom.*) is Mars. It is hard to dissociate this from the numbers of soldiers and ex-soldiers in Britain.

* Various native deity names on inscriptions (though very many inscriptions come from around Hadrian's Wall). Top four (not in order):

  MAPONUS, whose name includes a word for 'youth/son', whose *int. Rom.* is Apollo, perhaps in view of the latter's special importance for maturing youths. Maponus appears concerned with hunting (an aristocratic pursuit?), like his reflection 'Mabon' in the *Mabinogion*. Perhaps Loch- maben near Dumfries was named after him.

  COCIDIUS, meaning unknown, a Mars (war) or Silvanus (woods and…hunting). A cluster of Cocidius inscriptions at Bewcastle around 30 km NE of Carlisle indicates that this is where the place-name 'Shrine of Cocidius' belongs.

  BELATUCADRUS: *int. Rom.*: Mars.

  VITERIS, variously spelt through confusion with the Latin word for 'old' (*veter-*). Interestingly, no *int. Rom.*

* There are 66 other Celtic gods and goddesses often with only one inscription apiece. Several are known from Europe too – like Mogons, after whom the German city of Mainz (*Mogon- tiacum*) is named.

* Some portrayals of interest: a god with antlered head (the Gaulish Cernunnos); goddesses that come in threes; goddesses associated with birds or animals (particularly the horse, like the Gaulish Epona).

* Joints of meat and beer-tankards found in the graves of some Celtic chieftains; that of course matches the 'belief' in immortality (above, p. 50).

These notes on British religion show how fragmentary and limited our understanding of religion can be without a continuous literary tradition. Further study of British religion would nonetheless be of great interest, provided we do not forget to ask questions rather than simply heap up information.

Greece: a special case
Finally, a glance at a very different nation of the Empire: the Greeks. Long before they came under Roman control (204-146 BC), the Greeks had written books celebrating their culture and inscribed stone with dedications to their ancestral gods. This went from strength to strength wherever Greek culture prevailed: mainland Greece, the islands of the Aegean, the northern, western and southern coasts of Asia Minor (Turkey), the shores of the Black Sea, Sicily, and the coastal towns of southern Italy. And by the time of Augustus Greeks were dominant on the Syrian and Palestinian seaboard (which is why the New Testament was written in Greek) and in the Nile Delta; meanwhile in Asia Minor, Greek culture was seeping inland from the coast. In all these areas of the Roman Empire, you would find Greek religion with its calendars full of festivals to various forms of Zeus, Apollo, Athene, Hera, Dionysos and so on.

Pausanias' *Guide to Greece*, written in the second century AD, reveals how little Greek religion on the mainland had changed since pre-Roman times. Foreign cults have made little headway (Isis and Serapis perhaps the most significant), and despite some increase in appreciation for a rather carnival-like Dionysos religion (the same that emerged in Rome as the *Bacchanalia*, chap. 3, pp. 37-9) the land-scape is still dominated by the ancient temples of Athene at Athens, Hera near Argos, Apollo at Delphi and Zeus at Olympia. Con-servatism was also imposed by economic weakness on the mainland: few new temples could be afforded, nor in many cases could essential maintenance. It was a rare treat when the Emperor Hadrian com-pleted the great temple of Zeus at Athens, begun seven hundred years earlier.

Economies were stronger in Asia Minor, though there also little had changed: a count of mentions of gods in the inscriptions of Asia Minor reveals that the top ten are traditional Greek gods – and the eleventh, Cybele, is at least local. Perhaps now was the age to proclaim the virtues of your goddess. We shall see this in the 'aretalogies' of Isis (chap. 5, p. 69), but you did not need a new goddess for that, as Paul discovered when he offended the religious sensitivities of the Ephesians:

4.8 Realising that he was a Jew, there was a single cry from everyone which they screamed for about two hours: 'Great is Artemis of the Ephesians!' After he had restrained the crowd, the town clerk said, 'Men of Ephesos, what man is there who does not know that the city of Ephesos is the *neokoros* ['temple-warden'] of the great goddess Artemis and of the Heaven-fallen?...'

Acts of the Apostles 19. 34-35

The statue of the goddess is believed here as elsewhere in Greece to have fallen from the sky – going back to prehistoric worship of sacred stones, believed to be meteors, and showing just how long religious traditions can continue. Ephesos is vibrant in its devotion to its native goddess, revered not only for miles around but throughout the Greek world. Indeed, local piety was such that this area later became a major centre for the persecution of the Christians.

Overall, the gods of Homer (c. 700 BC) and the festivals that you will find in any book on Greek religion have lost no strength. And those that sought the highest peak of Greek religious experience continued to turn to the Eleusinian Mysteries, where at the peak of a nocturnal ceremony the initiates beheld something of overpowering significance (we do not know what): they were given hope of a better life after death in a ritual handed down by the goddess Demeter herself, when she lost her daughter and she too suffered:

4.9 What Greek, what barbarian was so perverse, so ill-informed...that he did not consider Eleusis a shrine common to the earth, and of all man's divine possessions at once most awesome and most gladdening?...As for all that may be viewed there, this has been seen in secret displays by countless generations of happy men and women.

AELIUS ARISTIDES, *Eleusinian Discourse* 2-3

Imperial cult

So far, we have been looking at local cults – of Celts and of Greeks, and the accepted traditions of these nations. To these we now add new cults installed or encouraged at the beginning of the Empire, using religious practice to express adherence to Rome, its values and its government. In this section we look at imperial cults – worship of the emperor or his family – and the associated cult of the goddess 'Roma'. In the next section come 'official' cults – provincial worship of the principal gods of the Roman state.

Republican backcloth

The Roman king, last seen half a millennium before the Empire, continued a tradition blending political leadership with unique religious authority. The Senate, the primary religious authority during the Republic, was his Council of Elders in origin; and the consuls, the Pontifex Maximus (with his Vestal Virgins in the Royal Palace, the *Regia*) and the *Rex Sacrorum* ('King for the purpose of Rites') all individually continued religious powers which must originally have been the prerogative of the king alone. There must have been a special aura surrounding the person of the king – maybe not so unlike the Egyptian Pharaoh. But the coming of the Republic destroyed the notion of a person with more sacred authority than others, except in the home where the *paterfamilias* reigned supreme (chap. 2, pp. 28-30). But what when Republic turned to Empire, when once again, after an interval of 478 years, Rome was ruled by one special man?

Augustus: beginnings, 31-27 BC

Augustus did not accept the title of *pater patriae* (father of the fatherland) until 2 BC, but he had presented his relationship to the state as something paternal and sacred long before. During the 20s BC Vergil was writing the great national epic, the *Aeneid*, and reflected Augustus' image in his portrait of Aeneas. *Pater* Aeneas has a special understanding of religion and is repeatedly described as *pius* ('pious', i.e. religiously dutiful), reflecting not only Augustus' care to rebuild temples (82, he claimed) but also his whole guidance of the state and its values.

As early as 30 BC, the Senate decreed that wine should be poured to Augustus' *Genius* at dinners both public and private, ensuring the Emperor became a real presence in an age before photographs and television. This measure and others like it were scarcely spontaneous gestures by the Senate: they were part of a policy by which Augustus defined his position. The same year saw the beginning of annual prayers for the Emperor and his family by consuls, priests, and officials in the provinces. The prayers may not be *to* the Emperor, but they give him a special role in religious ceremony. And the entrance of his house was marked from 27 BC, by decree of the Senate, with laurel trees and a crown of oak leaves, signs of constant victory and of rescue of his citizens (symbols and values cynically stolen from Sextus Pompeius, an earlier rival for power). Normally one would look to the gods for both victory and salvation; but now the entrance to Augustus' home looked as sacred as the entrance to any temple.

In 27 BC also, he ceased to be Octavian and became, to the acclamation of a supposedly adoring Senate and nation, *Augustus*, a term whose appeal to religious mystique defies translation: 'Venerable', 'Religiously-dignified'? The thoughtful Greek historian Dio was at least clear that 'it signified that he was something more than human, since indeed all the most precious and sacred objects are referred to as *augusta*'. Dio also claims that Augustus had really wanted to be called 'Romulus' – but it is difficult to know how far to believe an account of an intention that was never fulfilled.

It is in this context that the question of emperor-cult first emerges – from the principal Greek cities of Asia Minor in 29 BC.

Greek models
In the Greek East kings had been a familiar institution since the meteoric rise of Macedon under Philip II (ruled 359-336 BC) and Alexander the Great (336-323 BC). After them, the independence of the Greek mini-states counted for little: what mattered was the superpowers – the Greek kings who each ruled a third of what had been Alexander's empire: Macedonia, Syria and Egypt. The emergence of Rome as a world power during the Hannibalic War (219-201 BC) disturbed the fragile balance of power (now complicated by an independent kingdom at Pergamon), and as Roman forces entered Greece, they had an immediate impact on Philip V of Macedon (221-179 BC) and presently on Antiochos III of Syria (223-187 BC). This shift in power produced problems for the Greek cities, who now found themselves in the power zone no longer of a king but of a republic with a division of powers – between Senate, consuls, and ex-consuls (*consulares*) who continued in authority in order to command the armies which the Greeks saw. To whom therefore should prayers be addressed? Various king-substitutes were tried:

* Smyrna as early as 195 BC created a cult of a new goddess – 'Roma' – and established games in her honour, the *Rhomaia*. Others followed.

* Elsewhere constitutional experts created a different deity, of uncertain gender: the 'God' or 'Goddess Holy Senate'.

* Others refused to believe that the generals they saw were

not the people that counted: thus there was cult of
Flamininus, who in all senses displaced Antiochos. Much
later there was even cult of Sulla (c. 80 BC) in Athens, but
perhaps that was more a sign of things to come.

Against this background it makes sense that an impetus towards
emperor cult in the provinces came from the Greek East in 29 BC:

> 4.10 Augustus meanwhile, amongst other business, allowed
> precincts in Ephesos and Nicaea to *Roma* and to his father,
> Caesar, naming him the *Hero Julius*. At that time these were
> the leading cities of Asia [Minor] and Bithynia. These were
> the divinities that he instructed Romans living amongst
> them to worship. But foreigners (whom he called 'Greeks')
> he allowed to create some precincts to himself – the Asians
> in Pergamon and the Bithynians at Nicomedeia. That is
> where this started and under other emperors it spread not
> only amongst Greek nations, but also amongst all the others
> under Roman rule. For in Rome itself and the rest of Italy,
> no-one, no matter how great his status, has dared to do this.
> However, when they pass away, even there those that have
> ruled with integrity are granted various divine honours and
> in particular *heroa* ['hero's shrines'] are built to them.
>
> CASSIUS DIO, *Roman History* 51.20.6-8

This passage of Dio (who was consul in AD 205 and 229) is not easy.
First, though there is no reason to suppose that Ephesos and Nicaea
were put up to making this application, all the same they found a place
in an imperial policy that was already developing: the *Divus* Julius
Caesar was already an available part of the apparatus and Octavian
himself was moving towards a religious definition of his position.
Secondly, were the resident Romans just *allowed* to worship Roma
and the *Divus* Julius – or were they obliged to? And thirdly, Dio's
views of the restrictions on direct, unadulterated worship of the
Emperor may be true of the aristocracy at Rome, but elsewhere eager
provincials do not seem to observe such fine distinctions – and may
not have been meant to.

The Greek cities of the Eastern Mediterranean were already
organised as mini-states, known as *to koinon* – 'the community' of
such-and-such a city – and it was these *koina* that applied for the right
to build temples in honour of the Emperor and his family. In the
circumstances, the priesthood of Roma and Augustus was likely to be
the most distinguished post a local worthy might hold. But in the

Latin-speaking West there was no tradition of ruler-worship and often there was little organised local government and few cities. The arrival of Roman power brought trade, towns, cities, and local government united in cult of the Emperor.

Advanced Augustus, 12 BC-AD 14

The year in which Augustus became Pontifex Maximus – 12 BC – was also the year when a great altar of Roma and Augustus was built at Lyon in southern France; it was dedicated on the first of *August*. Beside it stood sixty statues representing the tribes of Gaul; and on it were depicted the propagandist laurels and oak-wreath (above, pp. 57-8). At either side figures of Victory held wreaths. For years before there had been occasional meetings of Gallic nobles at Lyon, but now they were to be organised into a *Council of the Three Provinces of Gaul* meeting annually in Lyon. The altar was their cult-centre and it was politically significant enough to ensure frequent appearance on coins.

This was the beginning of a series of centres of imperial worship organised from Rome in the newer, less developed parts of the Western Empire. Another was built at Köln to consolidate the intended expansion of the empire into Germany. But at Tarragona in Spain there had been sufficient local emperor-cult for it only to need the final upgrade to an operating system worthy of a Province.

Rome too was affected by the progress of imperial cult. Since 12 BC or so, official oaths had to slot the *Genius Augusti* in between the great state god, Jupiter Optimus Maximus, and the lowlier *Di Penates*. In 7 BC, the same *Genius Augusti*, as we have seen (chap. 2, p. 28), is added to the Lares at the 265 crossroads of the city of Rome in a reorganisation of the cult of the *Lares Compitales*. Meanwhile Augustus made other statements through new abstract gods: an altar to *Fortuna Redux* ('Fortune that brings [Augustus] back [from Syria]') in 19 BC; the *Ara Pacis Augusti* ('Altar of Augustus' peace') in 13 BC; a temple to *Concordia Augusta* ('Augustan Harmony') which Tiberius was allowed to vow in 7 BC and dedicate around AD 10/13, marking himself as Augustus' successor. To the same period (AD 6 or 13) belongs the altar which Tiberius dedicated to the *Numen Augusti* ('Godhood of Augustus') – to receive annual sacrifice from the four priestly colleges (chap. 2, pp. 16-19).

All that remained was for Augustus to be declared a god – as duly he was after his death: the *Divus* Julius now received a new companion – the *Divus* Augustus, with priesthoods for the imperial family, Livia and Germanicus. Subsequent emperors would be added to the list, provided of course they had not been ousted in a coup or otherwise damned, for the apotheosis of a predecessor is a statement of policy by his successor:

SUCCESSES: Augustus, Claudius, Vespasian, Titus, Trajan, Hadrian
FAILURES: Tiberius, Gaius Caligula, Nero, Domitian

Imperial cult evolved gently in the direction of autocracy over the next 300 years. Tiberius (AD 14-37) and Claudius (AD 41-54) professed restraint. But Gaius Caligula (AD 37-41) berated a Jewish delegation for sacrificing *for* him, not *to* him. Vespasian (AD 69-79) improved the efficiency and spread of the cult over the Empire. The imperial families gradually found a role too: Tiberius found Augustus' formidable widow Livia hard to keep in place – she became Augusta in Augustus' will, but her death did not make her a *Diva* until Claudius; Hadrian (AD 117-38) had Trajan's (his predecessor's) wife to thank for his inheritance of power – so she got worshipped as well as the daughters of Trajan. During the later years of the second century emperors became keener on direct worship while they were alive . The focus of worship was in any case moving obligingly on from the dead *Divus* (*sit Divus dum non sit vivus* – 'he can be a *Divus* so long as he's not aliveus', said Caracalla [AD 198-217] unlovingly of his murdered brother Geta [†212]), and stress moved from the purist *Genius* of the emperor to the emperor's *Numen* ('Godhood'). Some emperors even identified themselves with gods – Septimius Severus (AD 193-211) was portrayed as Hercules, and Heliogabalus (AD 218-22) as the Sun-god of Syrian Emesa (which was where his family came from). Finally, under Constantine (AD 312-37), Christianity ensured that the line must be drawn between expressions of loyalty and religious worship of the emperor.

The significance of emperor-cult
What exactly was emperor-cult? A self-seeking, blasphemous and cynical imposition on provincials? An imposition upon reluctant emperors by provincials whose competitions in flattery and abasement knew no bounds?

* No one believed that the living emperor was actually, in the full sense of the word, a 'god', with the possible exception of Gaius (Caligula), whose mind was disturbed. Domitian's

crushing of his underlings under the title 'Lord and God' (*Dominus et Deus*) should be taken no more seriously than Vespasian's death-bed joke, *vae! puto deus fieri* ('oh dear, I think I'm becoming a god!'). Yet many might believe that the soul of man is immortal and it might not be inappropriate to view the soul of the most special of all men as a *Divus* – a sort of god, if not quite a *deus*.

* For their subjects emperors were unseen forces who operated from afar; their power exceeded that of all men; and they could crush your state – or be its salvation, for instance in times of earthquake or famine.

* It was important to have a good track-record of loyal emperor-cult in case you ever needed it. But it also mattered to the well-adjusted community that its rituals expressed and demonstrated its place in the world, including its dependence on the emperor. In the Greek East in particular, where meticulous systems of festivals finely tuned the concerns of the community, a flourishing emperor-cult meant a vital aspect of the well-being of the community was comfortably expressed.

* Key members of local society found the imperial cult a useful addition to their ambitions and a dignified area in which to be accepted as a leading member of the community. This was of particular importance in the less civilised provinces, where participation in the imperial cult was the same thing as attending a council as a leader of local society and was a way of expressing adherence to Roman-ness and all its urban prestige.

* Though some early emperors made a show of restraining honours, the provinces found emperor-cult too useful a means of expression to pay much attention to restraint and the restraint itself was most likely a gesture of display (primarily for home consumption amongst the Roman aristocracy who alone resented the cult because the emperor was viewed by them as less distant and less great).

* Imperial cult was organised from scratch in the West by Augustus and was a necessary and deliberate part of imperial policy.

It is hard to be fair to emperor-cult when in our times we have seen repressive personality cults foisted on (we hope) unwilling nations. However, a more realistic, if modern, charge against the emperor-cult would not be that it was tasteless propaganda or even blasphemy, but that it entrenched local privilege and downgraded local cultures in comparison with the bright lights of Roman-ness. That of course was the intention: better that Gallic notables should meet before the *Ara Romae et Augusti* than that they should busy themselves with Gallic nationalism. Rome was not in the business of promoting regionalism.

Capitolia and official cults

Like other peoples of the ancient world the Romans from time to time created new settlements, 'colonies', in the image of the mother-city (*metropolis*, as the Greeks put it). In these colonies they recreated the heart of ancient Rome: this was its citadel (*arx*), the Capitol hill with its temple of Jupiter Optimus Maximus, Juno Regina and Minerva – the first and most important temple of the Roman state (chap. 2, p. 13). Thus in Roman foundations you would often find a *Capitolium* marked by its temple to these official gods.

So there are many *Capitolia* in the colonies founded in Italy during the Republic. But later in the provinces of the Empire it was not just official colonies that wished to use *Capitolia*. The province of Africa (present-day Tunisia, with a re-founded Carthage as its capital) was rich in them. This was an area which very much modelled itself on Rome, whose aristocracy was influential at Rome, and which supplied emperors such as Septimius Severus and outstanding men of culture such as Apuleius and Augustine. There was perhaps a difference between the Capitoline cults and imperial cult: the former expressed the national identity of the Romans, the latter expressed association with the power of Rome and appreciation of its benefits. But the *Capitolium* too would be dedicated *pro salute imperatoris* ('for the well-being of the Emperor') and either would do to expose the Christians for what they were: in Africa during the persecution of Decius (chap. 6, pp. 85-6), a *Capitolium* could be the scene for the renunciation of Christianity, by sacrificing to pagan gods, and cursing erstwhile heroes:

> 4.11 What is more, the lapsed are forced in addition to use
> their tongues and mouths – in the *Capitolium* in which they

had previously sinned [by rejecting Christianity] – to abuse the priests, confessors [i.e. those revered persons in prison awaiting execution for admitting Christianity], and virgins [i.e. those who had taken the pledge], and to curse the just and those with a particular reputation for faith in the Church.

CYPRIAN, *Letter* 59.13

With few exceptions (notably the major foundation of Constantinople) *Capitolia* were restricted to the Western Empire and mainly its more civilised parts. They are found, for instance, at Toulouse, Arles, Narbonne, Autun, Besançon in France, and (centres important in the later Empire) Trier and Köln in Germany. They belong to the Roman West not the Greek East, and to those parts of the West that feel truly Roman. They are present in Gaul, but 'evidence for the cult of Jupiter Optimus Maximus in the towns of Britain is all too slight' (M. Henig, *Religion in Roman Britain*, 84). Romanisation failed in Britain.

Chapter 5
New Wave

Although most people now as in ancient times are born into their religion, we tend to believe that we freely and individually choose our religion: it is, after all, our personal salvation that is at stake. This degree of individual commitment was not demanded by the religions we have seen so far – something which can seem frustrating, as though the Romans had no real religion.

This is where we come across the exotic and impressive religions that were supposed to have come from ancient cultures of the East, in particular the religions of Isis and Mithras. They certainly have a greater intensity and appeal to the individual. But we should be wary of regarding them as a stepping stone from paganism to Christianity: the idea that 'the Romans' lost confidence in their 'state religion' and so turned in droves to these new religions is quite false. These fascinating religions are a minority interest, as we shall see.

No ancient religion other than Judaism and Christianity was much concerned with the good life, either, or fired with missionary zeal and the desire to convert others, though they were aware enough of the merits of their gods and occasionally proclaimed them. Strangely, the central truths and ceremonies of the profounder ancient religions were sometimes secrets and it was considered a terrible crime to reveal these to outsiders, to the uninitiated. A profound 'secret rite' is the original meaning of the word 'mystery': the Mysteries of Mithras are not who he was and where he came from! This is the sense of 'mystery' to which Jesus refers when answering the disciples' question about his use of comparisons ('parables'):

> 5.1 'To you it has been granted to know the mysteries of the kingdom of God, whilst to the others (it has only been granted) in parables, so that when they see they may not see and when they hear they may not understand.'
> *Gospel according to Luke* 8.10

The place of mystery rites in the eastern religions may have been exaggerated but they remain an important part of their mystique.

Egyptian gods

Origins and spread

Egypt today most often means the Egypt of the Pharaohs: pyramids, mummies, hieroglyphs. We can see in our museums remains from the Old Kingdom (c. 2780-2250 BC) and from the New Kingdom (1562 -1085 BC). But Egypt had declined since then: in 332 BC it was conquered by Alexander the Great, and after that Egypt meant Greek Egypt. Its greatest city was Alexandria, the capital of the Ptolemies (Greeks all) until the last of them, Cleopatra, was defeated by Augustus at Actium (31 BC) and Egypt became the Emperor's personal possession.

Greeks and Romans (like many people today) liked to believe that there was some special sacred knowledge in Egypt, regarded hieroglyphs as more than just a clumsy way of writing, and thought that the package of gods that emerged from Greek Egypt and spread over the Roman world was genuinely Egyptian and gave genuine access to deep secrets. These gods were as Egyptian as Yul Brynner in the film *The Ten Commandments*: they have their Egyptian dress and cosmetics, but they deliver products for the Greco-Roman market with a Greco-Roman drawl. Even the language of the ceremonies was Greek.

> 5.2 *A priest brings out hieroglyphs in front of the hero of Apuleius' novel:*
>
> …from the secret area of the shrine he brought out certain books, marked out with unknown letters: some suggesting by various animal-shapes abbreviated words for ritual utterances; others protected from the prying reading of the uninitiated by the way their serifs were drawn – in knots, twisted into wheel-shapes, or in thick tendrils. From these books he declared to me what preparations were necessary for the conduct of the rite.
>
> APULEIUS, *Golden Ass* 11.22

EXAMPLES OF GENUINE EGYPTIAN ELEMENTS IN 'EGYPTIAN' RELIGION

* The *'ankh* knot. Hieroglyphs. Anubis' head. (All: below, pp. 67-71.)

* Shaven heads and white linen garments for priests. That's how you recognise an *Isiacus*. We hear twice of a man in danger of his life disguising himself as an *Isiacus* in order to escape from Rome.

* Ritual of opening up the temple in the morning, dressing the statue etc. (below, p. 72).

* Nice to get genuine Egyptians/Aethiopians (doesn't matter which) to perform or dance. The Emperor Caligula could afford to. And they look good on frescoes or mosaics (go well with crocodiles etc.).

Gods, powers and comfort
The package of gods was originally designed in the early third century BC at Alexandria where experts worked on mythology, iconography (how the various gods in the package would be portrayed in art) and ritual.

The Egyptian gods travel as a family and one priest may serve them all. Most often revered is the mother Isis, whom we will discuss presently, but not far behind is her husband Osiris, usually in the new improved version 'Serapis', as he is known in Latin (Sarapis in Greek). Serapis was originally an Egyptian merger of Osiris, the Pharaoh-god of the Dead, with Apis, the sacred bull of the Egyptians. But for the Greek market he had become another Pluto to reign over a Greek Underworld with the Greek three-headed dog, Cerberus. In addition he had acquired the healing characteristics of the Greek god Asclepius and the latter's knack of appearing in dreams to deliver useful instructions (hence many inscriptions state that a dedication has been made 'on instructions').

Their child is Horus (or 'Harpocrates'), whose infantile thumb in his mouth was reinterpreted as a finger held to the lips in mystic silence. And their most frequent attendant is the god Anubis, who keeps his jackal's head ('barker Anubis' in Vergil's unkind words), but otherwise is kitted out as another Hermes (Mercury), messenger of the gods and guide for departing souls on their way to the Underworld – complete with the *caduceus*, Hermes' special twisty wand. Much rarer is the gargoyle Bes.

Amongst Greek goddesses none had been more venerable than Demeter. Not only was she the goddess of women's festivals and of corn, but she was also (so the Greeks believed) the first to hand down mystery rites, the rites held at Eleusis near Athens which represented the peak of Greek religious experience. Isis became the new Demeter: she had a special concern for women, originated civilisation, had her own mystery-rites, even her statues were based on those of Demeter. So syncretism – equating one god with another – is part of the original design in the case of the Egyptian gods. Isis is meant to be Demeter (Ceres) from the outset. But it is a dynamic cult and at times we see a larger claim: the Egyptian gods are the real gods that lie behind the baffling numbers of pagan gods in the world. The cry went up (in Greek of course): *Heis Zeus Sarapis* '(There is) One Zeus Sarapis!' – as, for instance, on this inscription:

> 5.3 One Zeus Sarapis Sun World-ruler Invincible!
> To Zeus Sun Great Sarapis Saviour Wealth-giver Listening
> Benefactor Invincible Mithras in gratitude.
> > GREEK INSCRIPTION (Rome, AD c. 200), *SIRIS* 389

Isis is even *myrionomos*, her 'of the million names'. Some inscriptions actually list the countless goddesses she is also known as, but simplest is a second-century inscription on the base for a statue:

> 5.4

	(I dedicate a statue of)
TE TIBI	You to yourself
UNA QUAE	who in one person
ES OMNIA	are everything
DEA ISIS	goddess Isis
ARRIUS BALBINUS VC	Arrius Balbinus.
	Distinguised gentlemen*

*i.e. Senator-class

> > CIL X 3800, *SIRIS* 502 (revised)

Another important characteristic is the reflection of the family in these gods. Fathers, wives and children all have their place in this religion and this displays a humanity uncommon in our picture of Roman religions. Isis in particular strongly emphasises the dignity of women and the sanctity of marriage. It is no coincidence that women had a prominent place in the cult and that family crises found consolation in this religion:

> 5.5 Corellia Aigle, aged 21. This has been made for you, most marvellous woman, by your husband Dionyttas. Be of good cheer, lady: *do(ie) soi Osiris to psychron hydor.*

5.6 You (have left us), sweetest immortal child, everliving grief, Marcus Ortorius Eleutherus, aged 10yrs 3m 3d. *Doie soi Osiris to psychron hydor...*

GREEK INSCRIPTIONS (Rome, towards AD 100),
SIRIS 461, 462

'May Osiris give you the cool water', a hope for refreshment in an underworld seen too soon by one's young wife or son, and a consolation for the devotee from all-powerful gods intimately concerned for you. So Isis appears to Lucius in Apuleius' novel – in a dream in order to deliver 'instructions' below, p. 66:

5.7 I am here in pity for your misfortunes; I am here on your side and propitious. Abandon now your weepings, abandon your lamentations, cast aside your sorrow. Now by my Providence your saving day shines.

APULEIUS, *Golden Ass* 11.5

Isis has her differences from Demeter too. Her dress and that of her devotees' may be tied in a special knot, in the shape of the hieroglyph *'ankh*, the sign of 'life'. Her headdress often shows a disc – of the sun – surrounded by a crescent moon or a cow's horns ('cow, the fertile image of the goddess parent-of-all' – APULEIUS, *Golden Ass* 11.11) or two feathers (flight and ascent...of the soul?) and palm leaves (of victory): all are the same shape and each may imply the others. This is only the beginning. Greeks of the last centuries BC had developed powerful ideas of Fate, inescapable, and of the goddess 'Fortune' (*Tychē*), whimsical but potentially bountiful. Linked to these was the divine Providence – a Fate that plans for the best or the hidden hand behind apparently random Fortune. Isis was to be mighty enough to encompass these ultimate forces: time and again she is depicted as Isis-Tychē with the symbolic rudder and horn of plenty; in a striking statement (see below) we are told that she 'defeats Fate'; and Lucius is 'received into the protection of Fortune who [is not blind but] sees and by the splendour of her light illuminates also the other gods' (APULEIUS, *Golden Ass* 11.15).

A religion with such large claims was uniquely self-publicising and its shrines, among its many priests and officials, would have *aretalogi* – publicists at the sanctuary – who would tell (*leg-*) the virtues (*aretai*) of the gods in mesmeric 'aretalogies', some delivered in the person of the goddess:

Isis as one of her worshippers. In her left hand, the *situla* holds the cool water of Osiris. In the right, a *sistrum* to jingle. Note too the dress tied in the shape *'ankh*.

5.8 I am Isis, the absolute ruler of every land. I was educated
by Hermes and discovered writing, both sacred
[hieroglyphics] and public writing [demotic] so that
everything might not be written in the same. I laid down
laws for men and gave laws that none can change. I am the 5
eldest daughter of Kronos. I am the wife and sister of King
Osiris. I am the one who discovered crops for men. I am
the mother of King Horos. I am the one who rises in the
Dog-Star. I am the one who is called 'the goddess amongst
women'. For me the city of Bubastos was built. I separated 10
earth from heaven. I demonstrated the paths of the stars. I
drew up the path of sun and moon. I discovered nautical
matters. I made justice strong. I brought together man and
woman. I laid it down that woman should bring a baby into
the light at 10 months. I made it a law for parents to be loved 15
by the child. I laid a penalty on those unlovingly disposed
towards their parents. I, with my brother Osiris, stopped
cannibalism. I demonstrated initiations to men. I taught the
worship of the gods' statues. I founded precincts of the
gods. I ended the rule of tyrants. I stopped slaughter. I 20
made women be loved by men. I made justice stronger than
gold and silver. I made it law for truth to be considered
good. I invented marriage contracts. I drew up languages
for Greeks and barbarians. I made good and bad be
distinguished by instinct. I made nothing more fear- 25
inducing than an oath. I handed over the man who plots
unjustly against others into the power of him conspired
against. I lay a penalty on those doing wrong. I made it law
to pity suppliants. I honour those who defend themselves
justly. With me justice is strong. I am in charge of rivers, 30
winds and sea. No one is held in esteem without my
agreement. I am in charge of war. I am in charge of
lightning. I calm the sea and raise it in waves. I am in the
rays of the sun. I sit beside the journeying of the sun.
Whatever I decide is done. To me everything gives way. I 35
free those in chains. I am in charge of navigation. I make
the navigable unnavigable when I decide. I founded city
walls. I am the one called 'Thesmophoros' [law-bringing,
epithet of Demeter]. I brought islands from the depths to
the light. I am in charge of rain. I defeat Fate. To me Fate 40
listens. Greetings, Egypt that reared me!
INSCRIPTION, from Kyme (Asia Minor) *BCH* 51 (1927) 378

Rites

The rituals of the Egyptian gods are distinctive. Every morning the temple is opened, the statue woken and dressed (there are even special officials to do this, the *stolistai* or 'dressers') and sacrifice performed. This is in stark contrast to normal Greek and Roman temples, where ceremonies only took place at appropriate festivals, usually once a year – for the rest of the year the temple was closed. But the 'Egyptian' gods were in every respect more intense and demanding. There was a corresponding ritual of closing the temple in the evening.

We hear of two particular festivals. The first is a spring festival called *Ploiaphesia* (Greek for 'release of ships'; the Latin name is *Navigium Isidis*, 'Boat of Isis'). This was held, in the Roman West at least, on the fifth of March and, taken literally, marked the opening of the sailing season with the launching of a brightly decorated (reduced-scale?) replica of a ship, loaded with offerings, which was allowed to drift away out of sight. At least that is how Apuleius (11.16) tells it, seeing it, maybe rightly, as symbolic of new life – though the opening of the sailing season would be vital enough to merchants, who are generally thought to have been instrumental in the spread of the cult across the Greco-Roman world. It was a popular ceremony, whose colourful procession is imaginatively described by Apuleius, and inscriptions proudly declare that so-and-so has been a *nauarchos* ('ship's-captain') – i.e. an official in charge of the ceremony. This is a festival for those living on or near a coast, something true of a very large number of people in the ancient world, given the absence of fast or even adequate road transport. Obviously there is no reason to suppose a uniform, universal Isiacism in the absence of any international hierarchy: the Isiacs in ancient Hungary doubtless did not celebrate this festival, unless they made imaginative use of Lake Balaton!

The other festival is modelled on the Mysteries of Eleusis (see chap. 4, pp. 56 and 67-8) and like them takes place in autumn. It is the 'Finding of Osiris'. For three days his dismemberment at the hands of his enemy Seth or Typhon is mourned; then he is found by Isis and reassembled (apart from one particularly vital organ). This is the experience which is shared in some way by those who have been initiated into the secrets of the religion, maybe the *Melanephoroi* ('wearers of black') whom inscriptions mention: it is a death and resurrection, despair and new hope story. But again we must not demand uniformity – we are wholly unclear on whether Isis-Osiris mysteries were at all widespread outside the pages of Apuleius and Plutarch: ancient religions did not need a Good Friday and Easter story, though many branches may have had one.

Isis shrines were busy places with a battery of officials. Morning and evening ceremonies, processions, initiations, festivals, reciters of aretalogies, interpreters of dreams – and astrologers, statue-dressers, nauarchs, trierarchs, lamp-lighters, shrine-bearers, altar-bearers, fire-bearers, basket-bearers, scribes, as well as plain priests, key-holders and various attendants and curators. Not all at one place, but an impression is given all the same. And we should add to this something rather new: staying a while at a sanctuary while finding one's way. Older was the habit of eating together as fellow members of a religious club: at Pompeii, there were found not only chicken-bones but also the worshippers themselves, overwhelmed by a volcanic eruption more powerful than their gods.

Spread and significance
We discover where the Egyptian gods were worshipped by looking at the archaeological remains. It is generally believed that the cult was spread by traders, whose very occupation makes them mobile. So we can see that the cult reaches Delos very early and from there reaches the Italian ports, notably Puteolae and Ostia. This explains the early popularity of the cult in Campania, e.g. at Pompeii and Herculaneum. At Rome the college of 'pastophors' is supposed to have been founded around 80 BC, but, as we have seen (chap. 3, pp. 40-1), the cult was excluded from Rome from the 50s BC into the early Empire and only finally recognised by Gaius (Caligula, AD 37-41).

It is hard to reach firm conclusions on the social class of the worshippers. Clearly they could be influential people beyond the class of merchants as at Pompeii. But equally clearly, the cult never reached beyond major trading centres in any great numbers. Its greatest stronghold was central Italy, though of course Greece and the Aegean were receptive to a cult that spoke and thought Greek. It reached the south of France and Spain direct through trade (not via Rome) and early. In some parts of the Empire (for instance, Pannonia Superior, today's Hungary), members of the army contributed to its spread. Britain, as usual, is a desert: the one Isis inscription 'London at the shrine of Isis', *SIRIS* 751a) marks a jug with a pub's name ('The Isis Shrine'). For the record, the other three Egyptian religious inscriptions all refer to Serapis. Even where the cult was relatively popular, there is no reason to believe it occupied more than a tiny minority of the population, and certainly we must dismiss the idea that subscribing to Isis was in some way a rejection of 'traditional Roman religion'. No one rejected anything to sign up with Isis: pagan cults, unlike the great religions of today, were tolerant of each other – even if Isis at times believed she was more equal than the others.

Mithras

Meeting down the Cave...

The Mithras religion was quite different from that of Isis. Mithras was not one of a team of gods, he offered no place for women. He had no processions – only secret rites performed in excitingly gloomy underground or semi-underground 'Caves' – which people usually call *Mithraea*. Mithras and his mysteries were supposed to be Persian, but the extent of the contribution of real Persian religion, as of real Egyptian religion in the case of Isis, is very limited (see the table below).

Though Mithras came out of the East he had no impact on the Eastern Mediterranean. His first significant home is in central Italy and more evidence for him comes from Rome than from anywhere else. He is in fact the most Roman of the exotic gods, worshipped by select dining clubs amongst soldiers and in civilised central Italy and Provence. It has even been suggested that the details of the religion were put together in Rome itself – and certainly there is a surprising consistency in the religion from one place to another, given that (just like other ancient religions) it had no leaders with authority over more than one Cave – no bishops, ayatollahs, chief Rabbi, or Pope.

TABLE: MITHRAS AND PERSIA

* The god Mithra is found in Old Persian scriptures (the *Avesta*), but it is very hard to connect what is said of him with our Mithras.

* The major feat of our Mithras is the slaying of a bull; in Persian texts an evil demon slays a primeval ox and this leads to the creation of all animals and plants.

* Persia is the home of Babylonian (Chaldean) experts in observation of the stars and so in astrology, which permeates the cult.

* Occasionally we meet the ritual cry of *Nama!* – genuine Persian for 'Glory (be to…)' cf. *Hallelujah*, as in a caption on a late- second century AD wall-painting in a 'Cave' in Rome: 'Nama to the Lions! Protection by Jupiter' (INSCRIPTION (Rome, Sta Prisca), *CIMRM* 480).

The rites

The Cave in which worshippers of Mithras met was a dark rectangular building sunk into the earth, best with a vaulted roof – a type of building that only became possible in Roman times. It was not large (typically 10 metres by 4, the size of a through-lounge), and as dining couches were installed 20 would be the maximum for many Caves. Here they performed secret rites which seemed absurd to hostile outsiders (as with the rituals of Freemasonry):

> 5.9 Further, what about that ludicrous performance they undergo blindfold in the Cave? They are blindfolded in case their eyes shudder at being disgustingly degraded! Some, like a bird, flap their wings, imitating the cry of a raven. Some roar like lions. Some have their hands tied with chicken-gut and are cast over pits full of water, whilst someone comes up with a sword and breaks this gut, who calls himself the 'liberator'.
>
> PSEUDO-AUGUSTINE, *Questions on the Old and New Testaments* 114 (Migne, PL 35.2343)

This frantic Christian is mocking the series of grades through which the worshipper might rise (see below). On joining he would be a *Raven*, an attendant, a mere observer. Next he would be a *Nymphus*, a 'bride', ready (one imagines) for 'marriage' into the religion. The *Soldier* was therefore the first full grade, but we hear most about *Lions* – and that presumably is the standard grade. After that came more exotic and priestly grades. Rites could be picturesque, involving blindfolds, nakedness, kneeling, impersonating, even theatrical fake swords. Perhaps they could be brutal too: 'then they finally initiated him in the completer rites if he was still alive', alleges Nonnus the Mythographer (*PG* 36.989).

GRADES IN THE MITHRAIC MYSTERIES

Grade	Meaning	Protecting Planet/god	Associated Emblems
CORAX	RAVEN	Mercury	*Caduceus* (wand), raven, beaker
NYMPHUS	BRIDE	Venus	Crown, lamp, veil
MILES	SOLDIER	Mars	Pack, helmet, spear, arrows
LEO	LION	Jupiter	Thunderbolt, fire-spade, *sistrum* (rattle)
PERSES	PERSIAN	Moon	Half-moon, Persian sword, scythe, ears of corn
HELIO-DROMUS	SUN-RUNNER	Sun	Radiant crown, torch (raised), whip
PATER	FATHER	Saturn	Staff, Phrygian cap, sickle, ring

A ritual for the grade of Soldier was certainly unusual:

> 5.10 when being initiated in a Cave...he has a *corona* (garland, crown) brought to him on a sword...then has it fitted to his head, but is instructed to put his hand in the way, cast it from his head...saying that MITHRAS IS HIS GARLAND. Immediately he is considered a soldier of Mithras if he casts aside the crown, if he says the crown lies in his god. And from then on he is never garlanded and has this characteristic as a sign of his test.
>
> TERTULLIAN, *The Crown (of Martyrdom)* 15.3-4

A garland was a mark of great distinction for soldiers and generals – rather like receiving a medal. It was regular wear for priests too (like the Arval Brethren). But a commoner occasion to refuse a garland would be at parties, where garlands played the part of paper hats at Christmas.

The meaning and the myth

Lions represented the element of fire. Two of the three symbols associated with the Lion in the table above are connected with blazing fire. And on the wall of the Cave under Sta Prisca at Rome the 'Lion' is dressed entirely in red and his caption (is it part of a Mithraic liturgy?) reads:

The Lion grade as Mithraists saw it. His breath lights an altar flame, in his hands burn torches (held upwards as a symbol of renewal). His wings promise the ascent of the soul. Three elements – fire, earth (the snakes) and air – are strongly suggested. The fourth, water, is of course excluded.

> 5.11 Accept, Father, accept in holiness incense-burning
> Lions – through whom we give incense, through whom we
> are ourselves consumed.
>
> INSCRIPTION, CIMRM 485

The fire burns the incense, as it will burn our bodies when we are dead
and our soul is released, passing through the element of fire on its
ascent to the heavens. This is the fire that the Lions represent as the
incense is consumed.

For the Cave itself is 'an image of the universe which Mithras
made and its successive internal features symbolise the cosmic
elements and zones' (PORPHYRY, *Cave of the Nymphs* 5). Mosaic
floors depict an ascending ladder of grades with their symbols,
starting at the entrance of the Cave; its vault or roof (sometimes
decorated with stars) represents the sky, the rocky 'firmament' of
Near Eastern mythology (cf. *Genesis* 1.6-8). And at the far end of the
Cave, the focus of the entire microcosmic building, stands a stone
sculpture or relief – of Mithras slaying the Bull, what we call the
'tauroctony'.

The tauroctony itself takes place in a cave, watched by a raven,
just as Raven-grade newcomers to the rites might only observe the
ritual, not participate. Participation in the tauroctony is restricted to
a snake, a dog lapping the bull's blood and a scorpion attacking its
genitals. The bull's death seems to lead to creation, and the snake,
dog and scorpion in some way reflect the various grades. Mithras, as
he kills the bull, usually looks up and away – apparently to the Sun-god
with whom he is closely associated and for whom, maybe, he performs
this vital feat: the sun is, after all, in the constellation Taurus ('Bull')
in spring as life begins again.

In stone reliefs, other scenes from the story of Mithras are
sometimes depicted around the tauroctony: he is born from the rock,
he shoots an arrow – at the rocky sky so that there may be rain or at
a rock to release water. The bull is seen grazing, is caught by Mithras,
is carried away dead on his shoulders. Some of this is reflected in the
strange verse inscriptions on the walls of the Cave under Sta Prisca:

* Fountain shut in the rock which nourished the twin brothers
  with nectar.

* This bullock which he properly carried on his golden
  shoulders.

* And the most important (orders?) of the gods I have borne
on my shoulders and carried.

* You have saved us too by shedding the eternal blood.

Extracts from CIMRM 485

Place in the history of religion

It has been thought that but for the accident of history, Europe might
now be Mithraic rather than Christian – an entertaining thought, but
unlikely. Mithraism was always small-scale, esoteric and select. When
the Emperor Aurelian in the year AD 276 promoted an official cult of
Sol Invictus ('Invincible Sun'), Mithraists were able to satisfy their
loyalty to the regime by playing up the connection of Mithras with the
Sun-god and we find inscriptions to the God Invincible Mithras. But
this does not mean that Mithraism was official.

Admittedly, influential Romans worshipped Mithras in the later
fourth century, but why? This was the time of the last resurgence of
paganism in Rome. These aristocrats were protecting their identity
and high culture through elitist paganism. There was no question of
finding an alternative to Christianity for the general population. In
any case they had no success: Mithraists suffered at the hands of the
Christians. Literature and archaeology tell us that their Caves were
vandalised, and in the Mithraeum at Sarrebourg (Alsace) arch-
aeologists made a gruesome discovery: on the smashed remnants of
a tauroctony, a skeleton in chains.

So Mithraists were not competing for the souls of Europe in a
Grand Final with Christianity. But equally they were more than just
an idle and deluded scatter of dining clubs. In their exotic and slightly
masochistic way, they assigned their members a place in the universe:
they felt part of creation and its riches, they had a sense that efforts
were needed for the soul to rise from its present condition through
the real components of the universe to an ultimate association with a
power which they – and the philosophers – saw in, or compared to,
the Sun. If reflection on the human condition and the attempt through
real devotion (seen, hated and therefore certified by the Christians)
to escape its limitations are a valuable part of religion, then this
remarkable phenomenon in ancient paganism fully deserves its place
in the history of religions.

Chapter 6
Christian Toleration

There were several other cults that were not confined by national boundaries within the Roman Empire, but few as successful as the Egyptian gods or Mithras. In a larger book I would have included Cybele and her revolting *taurobolium* rite (rebirth by being drenched in the warm blood of a bull sacrificed above you...). Perhaps too Jupiter Dolichenus (popular amongst soldiers), Zeus Sabazios (whose devotees often left sculptures of hands, in a gesture of blessing – and crawling with symbols), and even the Syrian goddess (swirling dancing, flailing whips) or the Phrygian moon-god, Men, might have found a place. But one final cult cannot be left out: Christianity. Why?

If the persecution by Decius (below, pp. 85-6) had been success-ful and the cult had perished, Christianity might have had the same sort of interest as the *Bacchanalia* (chap. 3, pp. 37-9). As it is, following its adoption by Constantine in AD 312 it became rapidly more influential. With the crumbling of Roman political power in the West in the later fifth century (= 'Fall of the Roman Empire', a gradual process), it offered alternative social structures for the preservation of leadership and community in an increasingly unstable world ('the Dark Ages'). No pagan cults could have done this: they were not sufficiently organised, hierarchical or authoritarian. Today, of course, Christianity is felt to be a major part of Western European and American culture and any idea that it is in retreat before the advances of a secular world needs to be viewed in the light of projections that by the year 2000 there are likely to be around 2 billion adherents.

There are countless interesting aspects of Christianity in the Roman Empire. Here I look in a limited way at persecution, the conflict of Christianity with the people of the Empire and its government.

Christians as aliens

Nero: unwelcome recognition
The worshippers of Christ like those of many other religions were

soon established in Rome – capital cities attract more traders and cause more population-movement than other cities. The first step was their recognition not just as a splinter-group of Judaism, but as something separate. This appears to have happened under Nero, when, for instance, Paul attracted attention to the cult by appealing to the Emperor. The consequences (if such they were) were appalling: Nero found in these Christians useful distractions from his political difficulties, maybe including (as Tacitus alleges) the fire of Rome in AD 64.

> 6.1 But no human assistance, no grants by the Emperor, no placations of the gods could stop a report which led people to believe the fire was started on orders. To scotch the rumour Nero found people to blame and thought up exotic punishments for those people, hated for their crimes, who are commonly called 'Christians'. The originator of this title, Christus, was executed under Tiberius by the procurator Pontius Pilatus. This deadly superstition had been halted for the time being but broke out again not just in Judaea, the point of origin of this ill, but also in Rome – where everything vile and disgusting from any source collects and has its devotees. So first of all those who admitted to it were arrested, then on their information a vast number were convicted – not so much on the charge of arson as much as out of the hatred of the human race.
>
> TACITUS, *Annals* 15.44

Religion in the pagan world was for bringing people together and secret cults too respected the other pagan cults in which the wider community participated. The Christians, however, were separate, non-participants in the pious but enjoyable festivals of local society. When Tacitus uses the phrase 'hatred of the human race', we cannot tell whether he means that the Christians had 'hatred for the human race' or suffered 'hatred from the human race' – it makes little difference: they were socially alienated and ready victims.

Pliny and Trajan: rules

Much of the history of the development of Christianity is invisible to us. By the time of Pliny, it seems that practising Christianity was treated by magistrates as a crime. Some scholars think there had been some sort of law or edict against Christianity (for instance, under Nero), but Roman criminal law was chaotic and uncodified: if you thought a person had done wrong, you could report him to a magistrate and it was up to him whether he agreed it was a crime, i.e. worth punishing. This was known as a *cognitio extraordinaria* ['extra-ordinary hearing'] and bringing a case at such a hearing was technically a *persecutio* ['pursuit/suing'] – hence the word 'persecution'. As there was no police force, it was left to individuals to bring cases, to *persequi*; and this, of course, lends itself to abuse, as it becomes a way to make life difficult for your enemies or rivals. Pliny, as a Roman governor in Bithynia in AD 111-13, was unclear on how Christianity was generally handled:

> 6.2   GAIUS PLINY TO THE EMPEROR TRAJAN
> It is my regular custom, my lord, to refer all matters where I am in doubt to you. Who can better guide my hesitation or instruct my ignorance? I have never been present at hearings concerning Christians: so I do not know what is usually punished or examined or to what extent. I have had no little hesitation over whether any distinction should be made on grounds of age or whether, no matter how young they are, they should be treated no differently than the mature. And should pardon be given in cases of retraction, or is it no advantage to a person to have stopped if he has been a Christian at all? Is it the actual name [i.e. 'Christian'] that is punished if no crimes are associated with it, or is it crimes that are an integral part of the name?
>
> PLINY, *Letters* 10.96.1-2

Pliny, one of Rome's most civilised and well-meaning men if rather a slave to conventional values, gives his Christians every chance to retract. But if they will not, 'I ordered them to be taken away' (to be killed), unless they are Roman citizens in which case, like Paul, they are sent to Rome for trial.

But what to do if people are anonymously accused, the obvious way of getting at your enemies?

> 6.3... some denied that they were or ever had been Christians: these I thought it right to acquit after they had invoked the gods following my words and prayed to your statue (which I had ordered should be brought for the purpose together with the statues of the gods) with incense and wine, and in addition had cursed Christ. Real Christians, it is said, cannot be made to perform any of these actions.
>
> PLINY, *Letters* 10.96.5

Pliny has even made inquiries to discover what the religion is like, and after torturing maidservants – a routine barbarity in ancient legal processes – 'I discovered nothing but a perverse and exaggerated superstition'. This is not, of course, to pardon it, because 'persistence and unbending obstinacy must be punished' – and that means death. Given the lack of a prison system in the ancient world, penalties were few: fines, confiscations, exile (to an island), enslavement (in a mine) – or capital punishment, which was freely meted out, in particular to non-citizens. There is no point in fining a maidservant. By definition a slave does not own property – she *is* property.

Trajan's reply lays down a policy for the future:

> 6.4 You have followed the procedure you should have done in scrutinising the cases of Christians reported to you – there is nothing which can be laid down which would have any sort of fixed form and general application. They should not be searched out; but if they are reported and the case against them is proved, they are to be punished – with the reservation that a person who denies he is a Christian and makes this plain by action, i.e. by praying to our gods, should gain pardon from retracting, however suspect his past. But anonymous written allegations should have no place in any charge – they make a terrible precedent and are out of keeping with our times.
>
> TRAJAN in PLINY, *Letters* 10.97

A number of facts about the distribution of the cult also emerge from Pliny. It is interesting, in the light of the prominence of women and the underprivileged in the early church, that maidservants are found as officials of the cult. And though it is sometimes thought that it spread through country districts, it is perhaps more likely that the towns were the centre for it as for everything else and that it is a sign of its strength that it spread *from the towns* to the countryside:

> 6.5 Nor is it merely the cities, but even the villages and countryside have been contaminated by this superstition. But it seems it can be halted and put right: certainly it is fairly clear that temples up to now practically deserted have begun to receive crowds and that holy rites long interrupted are being revived and that meat of sacrificial animals is generally available, for which until now there had been practically no market. So one can easily work out how substantial a number of people could be set right if retraction were allowed.
>
> PLINY, *Letters* 10.96.10

Persecution by popular request

Between Trajan (AD 98-117) and Decius (AD 249-51) Trajan's policy prevailed. No persecution was initiated from the centre, but Christianity was a crime to be tested by refusal to engage in (pagan) religious observance. It 'should not be searched out', but it could be reported. So persecution depended on how local people felt about the Christians. As a result, persecutions in the Latin sense and in ours were sporadic. Christian writers have naturally found interest and inspiration in those who died for their faith and recorded them in as much detail as history allows: these are the *martyrs* who remained witnesses (*martyres* in Greek) to their faith and could not be pressurised to deny it. But numerically very few actually died and the impression that Christians were constantly being thrown to the lions, beheaded etc, is false. On the other hand, those who did die were sometimes treated more cruelly than other criminals, partly because of the defiance shown by martyrs.

To show something of the tone, we can look selectively at the martyrdom of Polycarp at Smyrna around AD 157. We see a crowd dissatisfied with just throwing a minor Christian, Germanicus, to the beasts: the cry goes up, 'Down with the atheists! Find Polycarp!' A posse is formed and though Polycarp tries to hide, 'the posse stayed at it and so he moved to another estate. Straightaway the posse was there and as it could not find him seized two slaves, one of whom admitted under torture where he was – it was impossible for him to remain hidden when his betrayers were his own servants'. On the way from where he is found the eirenarch (a sort of sheriff) and his father bring him to their carriage and try to persuade him: 'What harm is there in saying "Caesar is Lord" and sacrificing and so on and saving your life?' He refuses, is thrown out of the carriage and presently reaches the stadium 'there being such an uproar in the stadium that no-one could even be heard'. Polycarp, brought before the governor, agrees to shout 'Down with the atheists' but will not curse Christ. The governor

> 6.6 sent his herald to announce three times in the middle of the stadium 'Polycarp has admitted he is a Christian'. And when this had been said by the herald, the whole mob of pagans and of Jews who lived at Smyrna cried at the top of their voices with uncontrollable anger, 'This is the teacher of Asia, the father of the Christians, the destroyer of our gods, he who teaches people not to sacrifice or prostrate themselves.' This is what they said and they

shouted a demand for Philip the Asiarch [the top provincial magistrate, responsible for emperor-cult, for example] to let a lion loose on Polycarp. But he said he could not since the Hunt-games were completed. Then they decided with one spirit to shout for Polycarp to be burnt alive...The crowds immediately got together wood and sticks from workshops and baths, and the Jews were particularly enthusiastic to help with this – as they usually are.

> *Martyrdom of Polycarp* (ed. Musurillo) 12-13
> (= EUSEBIUS, *History of the Church* 4.15.25-9)

After he is burnt, the Christians are banned from taking his body 'although many were eager to do this and share in his holy flesh' and the Jews in particular prevent them from getting at the body. It is presently cremated and the ashes are handed over for burial.

We see reasonable enough officials, who try to talk sense into Polycarp, but massive local passions, focused on a stadium, whose crowd-psychology would bear comparison with political, religious and sporting gatherings today. This is Asia Minor where hostility to Christians ran strong: was the Church more visible there than elsewhere? Did the Greeks there have deeper religious emotions? They certainly suffered earthquakes and famines and it seems possible to link outbreaks of anti-Christian feeling with these natural catastrophes.

The account itself, of course, is not designed to explain pagan feelings except by implying wickedness, rarely an explanation for anything: it is a composition, or so it claims, by the local church for the 'information' of the broader Christian world. It ensures that martyrdom is recorded, glorified, garnished with biblical references (which I have omitted) and admired. No one records the numbers who did the sensible thing (a sacrifice and a few words), or went into hiding more successfully than Polycarp. It does not matter: the image of a community that can even feed on persecution has been created and is now a powerful tool. Even those who have admitted Christianity and are awaiting execution, the so-called 'confessors', have special religious powers – to heal and to forgive.

Persecution as policy

Decius: old-fashioned piety
The accession of the Emperor Decius late in AD 249 marked a turning-point. Persecution of the Christians now became government policy.

On the larger scale, it is clear that the crisis was at hand: without the high profile which intermittent official persecutions gave in the later third century Christianity would scarcely have been in a position to become the official religion under Constantine in AD 312.

Decius projected himself as a rock of traditional values and piety in an unstable world. He added Trajan's name to his own to mark his strength and traditionalism. And in religion he attempted to restore traditional practices and places of worship. His predecessor, Philip the Arab, is alleged to have had Christian leanings. Decius, by contrast, in a huge gesture to restore the *pax deorum* ordered all inhabitants of the Empire to sacrifice to the gods (whichever they were in your country) throughout the Empire. Only Jews were exempt from this decree. Furthermore, it was no idle decree: commissioners were appointed in every district to see that it was enforced. In cases of doubt, you were required to obtain certificates that you had always practised sacrifice in the past and now did so, tasting the victims before the commissioners.

Though the motive for the decree was a general one of piety and restoring the *pax deorum*, the Christians were clearly in the firing line – Decius cannot have believed otherwise and must have intended that through this edict the Christians would be brought to heel. At the least, they are scapegoats for the disintegration of Roman government and power during the third century (only reversed by Diocletian at the end of the century). At the most, they may have become significantly more numerous, more visible and more worrying to traditional piety and invited persecution by their growing strength, as their historian, Eusebius, believed. We cannot tell. Whatever the reason, this persecution seems to have been particularly effective, as bishops went into hiding and a realistic number of Christians obtained certificates (sometimes on the black market), becoming – to their shame – *libellatici* ('certificatees'). Only Decius' death brought it to an end (AD 251).

Diocletian: Restoration work

There were further persecutions under Valerian (AD 253-60) and Aurelian (AD 270-5), but the longest and most serious persecution was begun by Diocletian on 23 February AD 303. His religious policy was not so very different from that of Decius – or even Augustus. As Constantine later observed with puzzlement, Diocletian began the persecution at a time when peace had otherwise been restored to the

Empire. But this is the key. Diocletian now sought to restore the moral fabric of Rome. On 1 May AD 295, for instance, he promulgated a decree defining carefully what marriages were to be thought incest-uous and banning them. His reasons for this are religious and moral:

> 6.7 For in this way there can be no doubt that the immortal gods themselves will be favourable, as they always have been, to the Roman Name and won over, namely if we see that everyone who acts under our Empire cultivates a pious, religiously scrupulous (*religiosam*), peaceful and chaste life in absolutely all respects.
>
> EDICT of DIOCLETIAN, in *Comparison of Mosaic and Roman Laws* 6.4.1

If Diocletian can cultivate the *pax deorum* in a decree on incest, it is not unreasonable to view the decree on Christianity in the same light. We cannot continue denying that attacks on Christians could be motivated by the genuine religious and moral feeling of pagans:

> 6.8...the immortal gods by their providence have seen fit to ordain and dispose what is good and true in such a way that it should be approved and established by the judgment of many good and outstanding men of the greatest wisdom and be unimpaired by this treatment. It is not right [*fas*] to obstruct or resist this, nor should old religion be found fault with by new. It is the greatest crime to revoke things which, once established and determined by the ancients, hold and maintain their position and course. For this reason it is our earnest intention to punish the obstinacy of the perverted minds of utterly evil men. These men, who set new-fangled and unprecedented sects in opposition to the older religious practices, are using their perverted judgment to shut out what heaven once bestowed upon us...
>
> EDICT of DIOCLETIAN, in *Comparison of Mosaic and Roman Laws* 15.3.2-3

The object of this attack, on 30 March AD 297, is in fact not the Christians but the Manichaeans: others too were responsible for the religious malaise of the Empire. But the message is clear: the traditions of a very traditional nation, accustomed to look for its real values in a lost past peopled by heroic and moral ancestors, the men who had made Rome, are undermined by Christianity. The spiritual core, the piety and dignity and very identity of the Romans as a nation are declared invalid by this new-fangled cult.

We cannot go here into the detail of the persecution. Even its extent, though it lasted from AD 303 to 312, is unclear – emperors pagan and Christian had an exaggerated idea of how much could be achieved by their pompous edicts. The historian Norman Baynes showed how patchy and unclear our picture is:

> On one day in Egypt one hundred Christians were martyred: in Palestine during all the years of the persecution not one hundred were put to death. Of the extent of the repression in Asia Minor where Christianity was strongest we can form no impression. In Phrygia we are told a whole town was Christian: in the persecution it was surrounded by soldiers who under orders from the governor burned to death the entire population since none would deny their faith...but the student can hardly avoid the question whether both Eusebius and Lactantius did not mention the disaster suffered by this Phrygian town precisely because it was an exceptional atrocity.
>
> *Cambridge Ancient History*, vol. 12 (1939), 674

Christian restoration

In any event, the 'Great' persecution failed, either because it actually increased resolution among Christians, or because it was inadequately enforced, or because Constantine, growing in power, had through opportunism or gradual conversion begun to lend Christianity support, or because of loss of pagan nerve. As the Emperor Galerius, the principal persecutor, lay dying in AD 311 from an appalling disease rotting his body as he still lived, he issued an edict restoring the right to be a Christian (an edict signed by Constantine too):

> 6.9...we had previously wished to bring everything into accordance with the ancient laws and public discipline of the Romans and to see to it that the Christians also, who had abandoned the way of life of their parents, should return to good sense...But as very many persisted in their determination and we saw that the same neither showed due worship and observance of the gods nor kept up worship of the god of the Christians, we have thought it right, in view of our most gentle clemency and long-lasting practice [...etc....], to extend our readiest indulgence to these also, so that once again they may be Christians and hold their meetings, provided they do not breach the peace...
>
> EDICT of GALERIUS and OTHERS in LACTANTIUS, *Deaths of the Persecutors* 34

In the end the role of Constantine was crucial. On 29 October AD 312, he entered Rome in triumph – already adhering in some way to the Christian god. It was a useful act of policy to add Christians to one's supporters and it may also be that Constantine saw in the power of the Christian god an answer to the political turmoil he confronted in order to become Emperor. Stability was a crying need in AD 312 just as it had been when Augustus took power nearly 350 years earlier. The so-called 'Edict of Milan' (in fact a letter issued by Licinius after a meeting with Constantine which dealt only with a limited range of provinces) states the new policy clearly:

> 6.10...amongst the other things we saw would be of benefit to a large number of men, or thought we should arrange first, was the issue of reverence for divinity, so that we might grant Christians and everyone the freedom to follow the religious observance [*religio*] that each person wished, so that whatever divinity there is in the seat of heaven may become placated and propitious to us and to all who are under our rule...
>
> LACTANTIUS, *Deaths of the Persecutors* 48

Aftermath: tolerance?

A pendulum reaction against paganism might have been expected: would paganism now be persecuted? Constantine was at pains to deny it. But none of his staff might sacrifice; and the rich pagan temples were looted of valuables – gold plate was even removed from statues – for instance, to glorify his new capital, Constantinople, at the former Byzantion. His son Constantius went further:

> 6.11 It is our pleasure that in all places and every city the temples should be closed forthwith and that by denying access to anyone the immoral should be deprived of the possibility of misbehaviour. Moreover we wish that all should give up sacrifice. But if anyone should perpetrate any act of this sort, he shall be slain by the avenging sword. We further decree that the resources of the executed shall be claimed by the Treasury and that the rulers of the provinces shall be similarly punished if they fail to take measures against crimes. 1 December AD 346 (or maybe AD 354).
>
> *Codex Theodosianus* 16.10.4

> 6.12 We order that capital punishment be the penalty for those proved to have engaged in sacrifices or to have

worshipped statues. Milan, 19 February AD 356.
Codex Theodosianus 16.10.6

Such edicts were no more effective than the intolerant edicts of the pagan emperors. They are repeatedly issued, as Theodosius' edict of AD 392 or the following edict of 10 July AD 399 shows:

> 6.13 Any temples that are in the countryside should be demolished without trouble and commotion. For if these are destroyed and removed the entire material for superstition will be exhausted.
>
> EDICT of ARCADIUS and HONORIUS in *Codex Theodosianus* 16.10.6

To destroy a temple does not destroy devotion, though St Martin, had he lived two years longer, would have enjoyed this edict. The real battle is for a way of life, a way of living with one's world – conversion, not prohibition. In this, the severed head of St Julian (chap. 4, p. 53) was more useful than a cartload of edicts.

Meanwhile, looking from the Europe of the 1990s it is difficult to believe that civilized society and a peaceful world are possible without attempting tolerance and respect for views and practices with which we disagree, something which the pious vandalism of St Martin would never have understood. A large measure of tolerance was built into ancient paganism and it was as concerned as Christianity to approach the divine in a correct and pious manner. Indeed, we might – and should – respect these practices if they were current today and not condemned both to be 'ancient' and to be viewed as an unholy rival to nascent Christianity. The tragedy of Roman paganism was that it was so religious that it could not find a place in its world for Christianity. It has taken us 1600 years to recover the religious toleration briefly, if grudgingly, allowed by Constantine and glimpsed again under the short-lived enlightenment of Julian (AD 360-3). Let us hope it will not be lost.

Suggestions for Further Study

1. What are the basic features of modern religions? Would Varro's headings (chap. 2, pp. 14-15) work for a book on modern religions? In what ways do non-Christian religions differ from Christianity? How much do scriptures or mythology or performance of ritual matter? Is religion in the Roman world radically different from all modern religions? If so, in what ways and why? Would paganism be practical for Britain today?

2. To what extent did the Roman elite exercise control over religion during the Republic and during the Empire? What forms of religion were unaffected by their interest? What did they get out of religion for themselves? Did they have religious 'ambitions'? Must we regard them as insincere and calculating?

3. Look at Ovid *Fasti* (e.g. in the Loeb Classical Library translation) or Scullard's *Festivals and Ceremonies of the Roman Republic*. Select a festival or two that looks especially revealing about the Roman conception of gods or of religion in general. Explain exactly why – and suggest at what point it should have been included in the structure of this book.

4. Look at Livy 39.8-19 (Penguin: Livy, *Rome and the Mediterranean*) on the *Bacchanalia* (chap. 3, pp. 37-9). Why does Livy take the incident so seriously? What threats did it pose? Was it in fact pernicious, or is it gossip, rumour, bad press and mistrust?

5. Visit your nearest museum and find out what religious remains they have from the Roman period. What gods do inscriptions mention? Are they Roman or native? Can you see – and understand – any of the abbreviations (chap. 1, p. 5)? Are there cult implements or statuettes? Is there anything interesting on coins? What can we learn about religion from these remains? And if you have the remains of a religious site near you, visit it, learn about it, envisage what it was originally like and what happened there.

6. How do modern rulers manage without Prime Minister cult? Is there a 'cult' of the Royal Family? Were the Christians right to refuse to worship the Emperor?

7. Look at Apuleius, *The Golden Ass*, Book 11 (Penguin, last two chapters). In what way is this Isis religion personal or spiritual? Is the hero just a gullible fool who is tricked into spending his money by salesmen of religion? Why is he prepared to spend all? What is the purpose of processions and what are their attractions?

8. Look at Eusebius, *History of the Church* (= *Ecclesiastical History*, in the Loeb Classical Library, 2 vols, or a paperback abridgement). How frequent and how widespread are persecutions? What attitudes does Eusebius wish us to think were shown by (a) Christians (b) Roman officials (c) pagan people? What problems were posed by Christians for Roman government? What different problems were posed by persecutions for Christian communities, and in what different ways did they respond? What classes and conditions of people were prominent in the Church? Do we learn what in fact attracted people to Christianity?

9. On what assumptions is it possible to be tolerant to other religions? Is tolerance a virtue or a failure? Is there any sense in the last paragraph of chapter 6 of this book?

Suggestions for Further Reading

1. Whole subject:

Oxford Classical Dictionary (2nd ed., 1970) is a useful data bank – though some contributors were rather old-fashioned, even for 1970. Entries under e.g. Pontifex, Fratres Arvales, Clubs (Roman), Ara Pacis, Mithras, Christianity, and authors quoted in my text.

There are some chapters still worth reading in the first edition of the *Cambridge Ancient History*: A.D. Nock in vol. 10 (1934), ch. xv 'Religious developments from the close of the Republic to the Death of Nero', and in vol. 12 (1939) ch. xi 'The Development of Paganism in the Empire' supplies much worthwhile information, if in a rather non-committal framework of ideas. N.H. Baynes' essay on 'The Great Persecution' of the Christians, vol. 12 (1939) ch. xix, is a readable account that makes convincing sense. At the time of writing the second edition was beginning to appear, with an essay by J.A. North on the earlier Republic in vol. 7.2 (1990) and one by S.R.F. Price on 'The Place of Religion: Rome under Augustus' in the imminent vol. 10.

M. Beard, J.A. North and S.R.F. Price are at work on 2 volumes on Roman religion from earliest times to the fourth century AD, one of text, one of sources (Cambridge University Press, c. 1996). There will be useful material too in J. Bremmer, *Encyclopaedia of Ancient Religions* (Routledge, c. 1995).

2. Old Roman religion:

R.M. Ogilvie, *The Romans and their Gods in the Age of Augustus* (Chatto & Windus, 1969) is an agreeable, informative snapshot of the profile of Roman religion, but it did not get to grips with the problems. H.H. Scullard, *Festivals and Ceremonies of the Roman Republic* (Thames and Hudson, 1981) contains a particularly helpful opening essay on the nature of Roman religion, but mainly consists of a well-written run through the religious year. By about August one wonders what the point is. More clearly purposeful and a mine of information is the venerable tome of W. Warde Fowler, *The Religious Experience of the Roman People* (Macmillan, 1911), though its ideas can be Edwardian – far too much fertility, magic and taboo.

G. Dumézil's *Archaic Roman Religion* (2 vols, Chicago, 1970) is tough going and not wholly safe. Vol. 1 is for the careful specialist; but vol. 2 is helpful on the Hannibalic War and on religious institutions.

3. Politics:

J.H.W.G. Liebeschuetz, *Continuity and Change in Roman Religion* (Oxford, 1979) is unfashionably interested in the elite – big names and philosophies. But there is an admirable account of the late Republic and chapters well worth reading on Augustus and on the conversion of Constantine. More persistent is the politically well-informed account of A. Wardman, *Religion and Statecraft among the Romans* (Granada, 1982), which ranges from the Hannibalic War to the end of paganism.

Somewhere here fit the insights of M. Beard and J.A. North, *Pagan Priests* (Duckworth, 1990), who make the barrier between religion and politics seem rather a recent invention.

4. Local and oriental religions in the provinces:

It is not easy to come by careful and complete accounts of religion in the provinces: M. Henig, *Religion in Roman Britain* (Batsford, 1984) is a marvellous achievement, but on a second reading (as is justifiable) says more about things Roman than things native. Anne Ross' *Pagan Celtic Britain* (Routledge and Kegan Paul, 1967), though sometimes overambitious, should be set alongside Henig. Perhaps Gaul is an interest primarily of the French, but ch. 6 of P. MacKendrick, *Roman France* (Bell, 1971) gives an enthralling glimpse of sanctuaries and springs.

On the eastern religions, the romantic, old-fashioned views of F. Cumont, *The Mysteries of Mithra* and *Oriental Religions in Roman Paganism* (both occasionally available in Dover paperback), were well-informed for their day and have exercised a great influence. This continued as late as R.E. Witt, *Isis in the Graeco-Roman World* (Thames and Hudson, 1970) and J. Ferguson, *The Religions of the Roman Empire* (Thames and Hudson, 1970). In the meantime, A.D. Nock, *Conversion* (Oxford, 1933, frequently reprinted), was more resistant than most to the imposition of 20th-century spirituality on these cults and explored issues of real religious value. Nowadays, we see that the complex pattern of ancient paganism requires books with a wider, but detailed, view, like R. MacMullen, *Paganism in the Roman Empire* (Yale U.P. paperback 1981) and W. Burkert, *Ancient MysteryCults* (Harvard U.P. paperback 1987).

5. Emperor cult:

The standard work, starting with kings in the Greek East but not really going beyond Augustus, is L.R. Taylor, *The Divinity of the Roman Emperor* (American Philological Association, 1931). S.R.F. Price, *Rituals and Power: The Roman Imperial Cult in Asia Minor* (Cambridge, 1984, also paperback) is of wider significance than its title implies and argues remarkably firmly that the view that emperor cult is a political debasement of religion mistakes the nature of ancient religion.

6. Christianity:

The need for a modern, pagan exploration of Christianity was almost supplied by R. Lane Fox's extensive and slightly wilful *Pagans and Christians* (Penguin, 1988), whose focus is on the Eastern Empire. Those preferring a more limited, chronological and 'respectful' approach will continue to admire W.H.C. Frend, *Martyrdom and Persecution in the Early Church* (Blackwell, Oxford, 1965), even if it has been criticised for a certain amount of historical inaccuracy.

7. For those with access to university libraries:

Standard repertoire of data: G. Wissowa, *Religion und Kultus der Römer* (Munich, 1902); update, not always credible: K. Latte, *Römische Religionsgeschichte* (Munich, 1960). Advanced, if at times risky, study of gods in the Republic: G. Radke, *Zur Entwicklung der Gottesvorstellung und der Gottesverehrung in Rom* (Darmstadt, 1987). Extremely reliable basic synthesis: J. le Gall, *La religion romaine de l'époque de Caton l'Ancien au règne de l'empereur Commode* (Paris,

1975). Recommended on the development of religion during the Republic: J. Scheid, *Religion et piété à Rome* (Paris, 1985). Many interesting contributions on religion, in various languages, are to be found in *Aufstieg und Niedergang der Römischen Welt* e.g. II Principat, vols 16-18 – look, for instance, at R. Beck, 'Mithraism since Franz Cumont' in vol. 17.4, 2002-2112.

Ancient Sources and Inscriptions Quoted

Who's Who

AELIUS ARISTIDES (AD 117-c. 187) arguably the greatest of the Sophists (public speakers) of the 2nd century AD, who could speak for Greece and its heritage.

APULEIUS (c. AD 125-c. 170) virtuoso Latin public speaker, who wrote a novel, *The Golden Ass*, which ends with the initiation of the hero in the cult of Isis.

AUGUSTINE (AD 354-430) key figure in the history of Christianity, voluminous writer of Christian treatises, especially the *City of God* in which he argues that the sack of Rome by the Visigoths in 410 was not the result of the rejection of the *pax deorum* by Christians.

PSEUDO-AUGUSTINE collections of works by famous authors sometimes accidentally include works by other authors. In this case, the *Questions on Old and New Testaments* is not really by Augustine, but another Christian of his time or a little later.

AUGUSTUS (63 BC-AD 14) towards the end of his reign had a list of his achievements (*Res Gestae*) set up in stone all over the Empire.

AUSONIUS (c. AD 310-c. 395) teacher, professor, poet, who recalled in his *Professors of Bordeaux* notable professors he had known.

CATO (234-149 BC) statesman and writer, a conservative who upheld traditional Roman values even when writing about agriculture.

CAESAR (100-44 BC) statesman and reformer, who described his military achievements in his books on the *Gallic War* and the *Civil War*.

CASSIUS DIO (c. AD 160-c. 235) a Greek who was consul around 205

97

and again in 229 and wrote a stylish and knowledgeable history of Rome up to his own times.

CICERO (106-43 BC) best known Roman, who rose through oratory to statesmanship and wrote (among much else) works of philosophy which touch on religion and theology.

CYPRIAN (c. AD 200-258) Bishop of Carthage, martyred in 258. His *Letters* deal especially with problems arising from the persecution by Decius.

DIONYSIOS OF HALIKARNASSOS (taught in Rome 30-8 BC) Greek professor of public speaking and literature, who wrote a very detailed account of *Roman Antiquities*, on Rome's early history and customs – the Greek equivalent of Livy.

EUSEBIUS (c. AD 265-c. 340) pieced together a history of the rise and persecution of Christianity up to his own times.

FESTUS (late 2nd century AD) abridged a work *On the Significance of Words* – halfway between a dictionary and an encyclopaedia – by Verrius Flaccus (early 1st century AD) and was in his turn abridged by Paulus (8th century). Life is too short for long books.

GAIUS (2nd century AD) teacher of law: his *Institutes* was the original legal textbook.

LACTANTIUS (c. AD 240-c. 320) lived to see Christianity adopted by Constantine; defended Christianity against criticism in his *Divine Institutes*, and revelled in the *Deaths of the Persecutors*.

LIVY (c. 59 BC-c. AD 17) contemporary of Augustus who wrote a 142-book history of Rome from its foundation, paying attention, for instance, to religious institutions.

LUCRETIUS (died 55 BC) left unfinished at his death an epic-didactic poem outlining and colouring the scientific philosophy of the Greek writer, Epicurus.

OVID (43 BC-AD 17) sophisticated poet known best for his love-poetry and mythological epic the *Metamorphoses* – but he also wrote a description of the festivals that made up the Roman calendar, unfinished when he was sent into exile for some indiscretion in AD 8.

PAUL (died c. AD 60) leading early Christian who played a large part in defining the doctrines of Christianity in letters which form part of the *New Testament*.

PAULUS see FESTUS.

PLAUTUS (c. 250-184 BC) adapted Greek comedy for Roman culture.

PLINY (AD 61/2-c. 112) statesman and landowner, published much of his correspondence, including letters to the Emperor Trajan, some of whose replies are also included in the collection.

PLUTARCH (c. AD 46-after 120) Greek philosopher, who also wrote many biographies of famous men from Greek and Roman history.

POLYBIOS (c. 200-c. 118 BC) Greek statesman, detained at Rome for many years – but in the best circles. Wrote a 40-book history explaining the rise of Rome to the Greek world.

PORPHYRY (AD 234-c. 304/5) Greek Neoplatonist philosopher, pupil of the great Plotinos. Wrote a refutation of Christianity. Deeply into mysticism and symbols – like his interpretation of the 'Cave of the Nymphs'... an image of the universe...

SERVIUS (born c. AD 370) wrote notes explaining the works of Vergil, line by line.

SUETONIUS (born c. AD 69) man of learning, wrote biographies of the emperors up to Domitian (81-96), leaving out no scandal that might reveal the 'true' character of his subject.

SULPICIUS SEVERUS (born c. AD 363) wrote an adulatory biography of St Martin without even waiting until he was dead.

TACITUS (c. AD 55/6-after 113) statesman and writer with snappy, withering style deployed at the expense of many emperors in his *Histories* and *Annals*.

TERENCE (before 185-159 BC) adapted Greek comedy for the Roman stage.

TERTULLIAN (c. AD 160-after 220) a master of Latin rhetoric, converted to Christianity and raged thereafter against pagans.

VALERIUS MAXIMUS wrote in the early 30s AD a reference book for writers and speakers containing remarkable events/sayings.

VARRO (116-27 BC) Rome's greatest scholar, see pp. 13-15.

VERGIL (70-19 BC) Rome's greatest poet. His epic, the *Aeneid*, summed up the values of his times, as well as those of his political friends (e.g. Augustus), and took a philosophical view of what it was to be a Roman and to act for the best.

What's What

BCH *Bulletin de correspondance hellénique*: French journal keeping us up-to-date, for instance, with new inscriptions.

CIL *Corpus Inscriptionum Latinarum*: a set of huge volumes attempting to contain every Latin inscription that is known.

CIMRM Vermaseren, M.J., *Corpus Inscriptionum et Monumentorum Religionis Mithriacae* (2 vols, The Hague, 1956, 1960) is intended to contain all inscriptions relating to the cult of Mithras and a brief account of every Mithraic item – building, relief, cult object or whatever.

RIB Collingwood, R.G. and Wright, R.P., *The Roman Inscriptions of Britain* (Vol. 1, Oxford, 1965) – and that's what it contains.

SIRIS Vidman, L., *Sylloge Inscriptionum Religionis Isiacae et Sarapiacae* (Berlin, 1969) collects all the inscriptions for the cult of Isis and Serapis (except the island of Delos).

Acts of the Apostles and *Gospel According to Luke* are books which came to be part of the Christian *New Testament*.

Codex Theodosianus (AD 438) collected decrees issued by emperors from Constantine onwards.

Comparison of Mosaic and Roman Laws (c. AD 350-400): Bible and Rome have same law – read all about it!

Laws of the Twelve Tables (451-50 BC) were the earliest law-code of Rome.

Index of Key Terms

aedicula 30
anthropomorphism viii, 26
aretalogy 69
augurium 16-17
augustus 58
auspicium 17
bellum iustum 23
blood sacrifice 2
caduceus 67
Capitolium 63-4
divus 59, 60, 61, 62
do ut des 3
ex voto 7, 52
fas 17, 25
fetiales 23
flamen 18
genius 7, 28-30
iconography 67
idolatry 46
incubation 52
inscription 10
interpretatio Romana 46-7
lar 27-30
lararium 30
lectisternium 32-3

libellaticus 86
martyr 84
Mithraeum 74
numen vii
paganus 46
paterfamilias 28-30
pax deorum 3
penates 25-7
persecutio 82
piaculum 3
polytheism 46
pontifex 18-19
religio 6
sacer 5-6
Sacred Spring 35
sacrificium 6
sellisternium 36
Sibylline Books 32
sodalitas 19
supplicatio 35
syncretism 68
templum 17
tripudium 21
ver sacrum 35
vow 7

Current and forthcoming titles in the Classical World Series

Aristophanes and his Theatre of the Absurd, Paul Cartledge
Art and the Romans, Anne Haward
Athens and Sparta, S. Todd
Athens under the Tyrants, J. Smith
Attic Orators, Michael Edwards
Augustan Rome, Andrew Wallace-Hadrill
Cicero and the End of the Roman Republic, Thomas Wiedemann
Classical Archaeology in the Field: Approaches,
    S.J. Hill, L. Bowkett and K.A. & Diana Wardle
Classical Epic: Homer and Virgil, Richard Jenkyns
Democracy in Classical Athens, Christopher Carey
Environment and the Classical World, Patricia Jeskins
Greece and the Persians, John Sharwood Smith
Greek and Roman Medicine, Helen King
Greek Architecture, R. Tomlinson
Greek Tragedy: An Introduction, Marion Baldock
Julio-Claudian Emperors, T. Wiedemann
Lucretius and the Didactic Epic, Monica Gale
Morals and Values in Ancient Greece, John Ferguson
Mycenaean World, K. & Diana Wardle
Political Life in the City of Rome, J.R. Patterson
Plato's Republic and the Greek Enlightenment, Hugh Lawson-Tancred
The Plays of Euripides, James Morwood
Religion and the Greeks, Robert Garland
Religion and the Romans, Ken Dowden
Roman Architecture, Martin Thorpe
Roman Britain, S.J. Hill and S. Ireland
Roman Satirists and Their Masks, Susanna Braund
Slavery in Classical Greece, N. Fisher
Women in Classical Athens, Sue Blundell